STRATEGIC THINKING AND THE NEW SCIENCE

PLANNING IN THE MIDST OF CHAOS, COMPLEXITY, AND CHANGE

T. IRENE SANDERS

THE FREE PRESS

New York   London   Toronto   Sydney

THE FREE PRESS
A Division of Simon & Schuster Inc.
1230 Avenue of the Americas
New York, NY 10020

THE FREE PRESS and colophon are trademarks
of Simon & Schuster Inc.

FutureScape™ is a trademark of T. Irene Sanders.

Designed by Song Hee Kim

Manufactured in the United States of America

10   9   8   7

Library of Congress Cataloging-in-Publication Data

Sanders, T. Irene
    Strategic thinking and the new science: planning in the midst of
chaos, complexity, and change/T. Irene Sanders.
        p.   cm.
    Includes bibliographical references and index.
    1. Strategic planning. 2. Chaotic behavior in systems.
    I. Title.
    HD30.28.S264   1998
    658.4'012—dc21   98–11329
                                                          CIP

ISBN 978-1-4516-2428-1

To my cousin
Judy Rutland Carlsen
(1940–1997)
whose love, laughter, and courage filled all our hearts.

and

To my clients
who helped me test and refine
the concepts, principles, and tools described in this book.

CONTENTS

Prologue

EXPLORING THE UNKNOWN

The most promising words ever written on the maps of human

knowledge are **terra incognita**—*unknown territory.*

—DANIEL J. BOORSTIN

The Discoverers

Ever since the first man stepped across the boundary of his known world and found food, the mystery of the unknown has lured explorers of all types away from their homes, families, and familiar surroundings. By land and by sea the early explorers set forth in uncharted directions, confronting fear and nature's obstacles.

Many, thinking that they would be the first to see whatever lay ahead, were surprised to discover human footprints, well-developed societies, and men willing to kill them. Others were indeed the first to chart a river's course, cross a mountain range, or reach a far destination.

The motivations for exploration—wealth, fame, greed, religious conversion, territorial expansion, or pure adventure—were as diverse as the people who followed them. But regardless of the motives, their discoveries expanded our view of the world and our relationship to it.

This expanding view of the world is recorded in the rich history of mapmaking. And the earliest maps were, no doubt, drawings designed to lead others to food or to prevent them from stumbling into a dragon's lair. They were artistic representations of what was known about a specific location and its geography. They helped one find his or her way through unfamiliar and perilous territory.

The spirit of exploration is alive and well today. Computer-enhanced compasses, telescopes, microscopes, cameras, and sonar devices are providing us with new information about outer space, inner space, and the oceans that surround us. It seems that every week new discoveries in astronomy, archaeology, biology, and physics challenge our assumptions and raise new questions.

Beautiful dreamlike photographs showing the birth of stars are giving astronomers new insights into the history of the universe. The discovery of an underground ecosystem in Romania with thirty new species of life is a dramatic finding. Cave paintings older than any previously known are causing scientists all over the world to rethink their theories about art, language, and the daily lives of our prehistoric ancestors. And new DNA studies indicating that Neanderthal man was not the genetic ancestor of modern humans are challenging scientists to rethink their theories about the origins and evolutionary path of human life.

The ancient and ever present question "Is anybody out there?" still captures our imaginations. The discovery of planets orbiting other stars, with conditions that could support life, and the finding that Europa, one of Jupiter's moons, also has an environment that could support life, put this question on the cover of news magazines around the world. Moreover, pictures from the surface of Mars reveal a rocky terrain that looks remarkably similar to the rock-strewn desertscapes found in the southwestern United States and in parts of the Middle East, giving us reason to ask "Are these images from Mars a reflection of our past or our future?"

When we turn our attention away from the heavens and back to Earth, we are forced to acknowledge that in many ways the planet on which we live is still unfamiliar and perilous territory. The Human Genome Project is ahead of schedule and already providing medical science with new diagnostic and treatment options, as well as raising important ethical questions about the uses of genetic information. And as Dolly, the first cloned mammal (a sheep), chews her dinner and looks into the camera, we are faced with new questions about the nature and meaning of life. Technology has brought us to an intersection where we are confronted with questions that are deeply personal and highly political.

But news of science's exciting discoveries and the profound questions they raise rarely make the morning headlines. Instead, terrorist activities, murders, and the latest upheavals in business and international politics scream at us as we down our first cup of coffee. The future already looks ominous at 7 A.M.

Ours is truly *terra incognita*. None of us have ever lived in the kind of world we live in today, and none of us have ever been to the future. So, each of us, in our own way, is a modern-day explorer. But, we need not fear that "dragons be here." A revolution is taking place in science, and it is helping us understand the complex and rapidly changing world in which we live and work.

This book is an explorer's journal. It describes my journey into the new science of chaos theory and complexity and the search for what it might have to teach us about the world of people, politics, and commerce. Mine is a quest to understand the nature of change and its relationship to the future, the dynamics behind the events we see and experience in our everyday lives. And the motivation for my journey comes out of my own curiosity and my work with government and business leaders struggling to shape the future through thoughtful and wise decisions.

In order to think and act strategically, we must first understand the context in which our decisions are being made. We need to see and understand the world as an interconnected whole, where our thoughts and actions influence and are influenced by many *unknowns*. This book describes my efforts to bring those unknown qualities into clearer view.

Like every explorer, I have added my own findings, thoughts, and assumptions to the notes of those who have gone before me. And like the early cartographers, I have attempted to use this information to create a map for future explorers. I invite you to go with me into this exciting new territory. Together we'll leave our footprints for others to follow.

T. Irene Sanders
January 1998
Evergreen, Colorado

Introduction

The only real voyage of discovery . . . consists not in seeking new landscapes but in having new eyes. . . .

—MARCEL PROUST

La Prisonnière

In the last decade, scientists attempting to understand chaos, complexity, and change, and organizations trying to survive them, reached the same conclusion: Chaos, complexity, and change are everywhere! Mastering them requires new ways of seeing and thinking.

The new *science of chaos theory and complexity* is providing us with information about the dynamics of change in the real world in which our decisions are being made. For scientists, the new science describes the orderly yet complicated and unpredictable behavior of nonlinear systems, systems like the ones in which we live and work. At the heart of the new science is the discovery that beneath what appears to be disorder there is order—a type of self-organizing pattern, shape, or structure that emerges through the rich web of tangles, connections, and interrelationships in the system being observed. And the most exciting discoveries relate to the *dynamics*, or "hows," of this process.

By applying insights from the new science to our lives and businesses, I believe that I have found a way to show you how to anticipate, respond to, and influence change as it is emerging and before a crisis arises. Through this new approach, I believe we have a way to reduce the fear and confusion we experience as we listen to the news and observe the changes taking place in our homes, our communities, on the job, around the country, and internationally. And at last we have a way to develop the much-needed skill of *strategic thinking*.

The new science is laying the foundation for a fundamental shift in the way we view the world, and with it the need for a shift in the way we also think about and do planning. My purpose in writing this book is to use insights from the new science to describe an exciting new model for *strategic thinking*, the first and most difficult step in any planning effort.

Until now, we have not had a clear way to understand the present, much less its relationship to the future. But with the new science we understand that the future is happening today. *The present is the future in its most creative state.*

ORIENTING OURSELVES

In a humorous article for the *New York Times*, W. D. Wetherell begins with the premise that "most people are direction-impaired."[1] This caught my attention, because most of the organizations I work with are initially "direction-impaired." Orienting ourselves in a world that is increasingly more interconnected and changing at an ever-quickening rate is a challenge even to those of us who believe that we possess an uncanny type of intelligence, known today as *geographic intelligence*.

Geographic intelligence is the ability to orient yourself in space and time, to know how a certain terrain is organized, and to use orienting tools to help you find your way through unfamiliar and often perilous territory. The ability to read a map or use a compass is a sign of geographic intelligence.

For the direction-impaired, whose geographic intelligence is not well-developed, modern technology has created the global positioning system (GPS), which uses Earth-orbiting satellites to identify longitude and latitude. The GPS is the modern version of a sextant, an orienting tool used by sailors to find their way through the open sea. This new technology has many land-, air-, and sea-based applications. In addition to the seafaring, airline pilots use global positioning systems to navigate in bad weather. Meteorologists use this technology to make weather forecasts. Farmers use it to make sure their fields are fertilized adequately.[2] Global positioning systems can even be found in rental cars, which will provide you with voice-synthesized directions to your hotel or meeting location.

Many other uses are being explored by serious engineers and GPS novices, who share an enthusiasm for this innovative tool. For example, on the day I bought my house in Colorado, a friend, George Long, escorted me to my new home with his new toy, a GPS. In addition to the traditional bottle of champagne, he also presented me with the coordinates—the unique longitude and latitude—of my new front door. So now, in addition to my street address, zip code, telephone number, fax machine number, and e-mail address, I can offer friends and business associates my longitude and latitude, and with the help of another friend, my altitude! At last, help has finally arrived for the direction-impaired.

However, the type of geographic intelligence required in business is out of this technology's reach. A GPS cannot orient you or your business in today's global business environment. We must find other ways to help ourselves.

The relationship of geographic intelligence to the material presented in this book struck me one day while attending a legislative hearing on the subject of standards-based education. Standards-based education is a new approach in elementary and high school education. It attempts to answer the question "What should students know and be able to do at the completion of grades 4, 8 and 12?"[3] The hearing I attended just happened to be on the topic of geography standards.

Geographers focus on the patterns of organization found around the world, and there are two perspectives that help make these patterns recognizable: spatial, that is, the placement of objects in time and space; and ecological, which recognizes Earth as "a complex system of interacting physical and human forces."[4]

Using these two perspectives, the National Geographic Society has worked with educators to develop a list of standards and skills by which to encourage and test the development of geographic intelligence. Each standard completes the sentence "The geographically informed student knows and understands . . ."[5] For example (I'll use "person or organization" instead of student), the geographically informed person or organization understands and knows how to:

- Use maps and other geographic representations, tools, and technologies to acquire, process, and report information;
- Use mental maps to organize information about people, places, and environments;
- Recognize global patterns and networks of economic interdependencies; and,
- Apply geography to interpret the present and plan for the future.[6]

In other words, the geographically informed person or organization knows how to see, think about, and interpret connections, relationships, and patterns of interaction, locally and globally. This book will help you do just that. It will show you how to develop the type of geographic intelligence needed in today's business world. It will show you how to develop a global positioning mindset in your organization, one that will help you navigate your way to a successful future.

WHO WILL FIND THIS BOOK MOST USEFUL

Because the concepts, principles, and tools presented in this book describe a new context as well as a new process for decision-making, it will be especially useful to:

- Chief executive officers, executive teams or boards, managers, and others who have the responsibility for thinking and planning strategically for the future of their organizations;
- Trainers, educators, and consultants interested in integrating the new science into their research and work with organizational change;
- Individuals contemplating major life or career changes; and
- Anyone who would like to learn more about the new science and its applications to their life and/or work.

HOW THIS BOOK IS ORGANIZED

This book describes a new model for *strategic thinking*. The *context* in which strategic thinking must take place is the global environment. The new science describes the *dynamics* of change in this global context. And there are *seven principles* for strategic thinking within the global context as defined by the new science.

Strategic thinking has two major components: *insight about the present* and *foresight about the future*. *Visual thinking* is the process that stimulates both of these by helping us link our intuitive sense of events in the world with our intellectual understanding. And a *FutureScape*™ is the tool that supports visual thinking. When we put all of this together we have the framework for the *new planning paradigm*, as defined by the new science.

The book is organized into two parts. Part One, Understanding and Using the New Science, explores the history of science from the perspective of change and explains the origins of our current preference for linear, mechanistic thinking, as well as the limitations of this worldview (Chapter 1); the modern scientific context in which the new science began to take shape and its basic elements (Chapter 2); and the first steps toward applying findings from the new science to the sociopolitical world and the seven principles of strategic thinking as defined by the new science (Chapter 3).

Part Two, The Art and Science of Visual Thinking, describes the process of visual thinking and the importance of developing our ability to use it as a way to see and understand the multiple complexities that are creating the dynamics of the real world context in which our decisions are being made (Chapter 4); a new tool, a FutureScape™, that supports visual thinking and facilitates our ability to develop insight about the present and foresight about the future (Chapter 5); and The New Planning Paradigm as Defined by the New Science (Chapter 6).

A Personal Journey To and Through the New Science

The course of my research and thinking about the nature of change began to take shape in the early 1980s, when I moved from Atlanta to Washington, DC, to serve on the legislative staff of U.S. Senator Sam Nunn. At that time in my life I believed that if I really wanted to make a difference in the world I had to be in a place where I would have access to information, ideas, and people on a grand scale.

Working on "the Hill" was exhilarating, exhausting, and one of the best learning experiences I've ever had. What I began to learn, however, was that in addition to our many successes there were other times when our efforts fell short of the long-lasting benefits we expected. There was often a disconnect between our intentions and the results. World events and national crises frequently pushed other issues aside, restructured political alliances, and rearranged budget priorities. Issues seemed to emerge out of nowhere. And very few concerns were ever taken care of once and for all. In other words, *what we thought would change almost never did, yet change was constant and often unexpected.*

Now I understand that there were two major reasons for this paradox. First, we did not understand the *dynamics* of change in a realistic and coherent way. And second, even though we talked about systems—the economic system, the health care system, our national security system—our perspective was limited. We did not see the *whole picture*. What we were missing was an understanding about the dynamics of change in the "big picture" context in which our decisions were being made. And our experience was not unique.

I began to read everything I could find about change, planning, global thinking, art, and psychology. I read across many disciplines and searched the international journals. I found a lot of interesting material, which pushed my thinking forward, but something was always missing. I never felt satisfied that the picture I had was big enough nor the depth of knowledge deep enough to answer my questions.

This feeling was reinforced over the next few years, as I started a consulting practice, focused on strategic planning and communications, and encountered the same questions over and over with my clients and their organizations. I experimented with a variety of approaches to help myself and my clients see and think about the larger environment. I even started using an art pad instead of a legal pad for note-taking, because the paper was unlined and bigger and I believed that somehow it would help me see and think bigger. I always felt that there was another approach that I had not yet found.

In 1989, just before leaving on a flight from Washington to Los Angeles to facilitate a strategic planning session for a group of hospital executives in the public-sector, my friend and former director of the Congressional Institute on the Future, Judy Hayes Ellison, told me about James Gleick's book, *Chaos: Making a New Science,* and urged me to read it as soon as possible.

I read the entire book on that coast-to-coast flight, and by the time I arrived in Los Angeles I had decided to experiment with some of the ideas I'd had while reading the book. I called Judy from the hotel that night, told her what I was thinking about doing, and asked for her opinion. Her response was, "Irene, who knows if this will work. It hasn't been done before. So, if it works you'll know immediately, and if it doesn't, you'll know that too!"

Public hospitals, whose collective mission is to serve the poor and uninsured, are always squeezed between the dual pressures of budget limitations and an increasing demand for services. The next morning I started the planning session with an overview of the concepts I'd taken from Gleick's description of chaos theory and presented a visual model that I believed would help them see and understand more fully the changes taking place in their chaotic "big picture" environment. I wanted to help them to see crisis as an opportunity with leverage points that could result in positive outcomes for the people they served. In other words, I wanted to help them think strategically within the larger context.

That first attempt to use the new science as a context for strategic thinking was probably more helpful to me than it was for the participants, although a few, including Mark Finucane, who is now director of the Department of Health Services for Los Angeles County, understood immediately what I was trying to do. Mark even borrowed my first copy of Gleick's book and has yet to return it!

That experience set me on a path that continues to this day. I knew intuitively that I had found what I'd been searching for. I recognized immediately that the new science would be valuable to individuals and organizations as they wrestled with their own questions about chaos, complexity, and change. I knew that the applications would become clear. But first I needed to learn as much as I could about the new science. And using science to explore context was as natural for me as breathing.

As a child I learned to appreciate both content and context—my father is a physician and my mother, an artist. And one of my favorite childhood memories is from a family vacation to western North Carolina in which we made a day-long expedition to find a Russian artist, Jacob Anchutin, whose paintings my mother admired.

We found him living beside a gently flowing stream in a beautiful mountain meadow. Propped up against an old log and surrounded by wildflowers beneath a hazy blue summer sky was a still-wet oil painting of his meadow with an imagined log cabin in place of the old converted wood-paneled Ford wagon he called home.

Despite the beautiful setting, he was not well. He had the obvious signs of a severe staph infection; severe enough that my father, who always carried his black bag in the car, gave him an injection of penicillin and a prescription for a follow-up course of oral penicillin. He also got the name of Anchutin's local physician so that he could give him a report when we returned to town.

My father never intended to ask for payment. But Anchutin insisted on returning the favor. Because I loved the little painting, he gave it to my father for me in exchange for his "house call." That beautiful and touching gift of art, given in return for modern medicine, hangs today on my guest room wall, and is for me a reminder of the many personal, practical, and mysterious connections between art and science—between context, that beautiful mountain meadow, and content, what was happening within it.

I developed my professional interest in medicine and science early, and in the form that was most culturally acceptable at the time, nursing.

My brother, who came along four years after me, also developed his interest in the acceptable form and eventually became a physician. Looking back, I now believe that at some level I saw medicine as the fastest and most direct route to experiencing and understanding the mysteries of life. And I know that my mother's involvement in politics and community affairs, her love of history as well as her enthusiasm for interesting people and places, had a great influence on how I eventually chose to expand my interests.

I've always enjoyed challenges and extreme situations, so as a nursing student at Duke University I specialized in psychiatry, while taking as many electives as possible outside my discipline in subjects such as anthropology, philosophy, and international affairs. And later in graduate school I focused on community health, health policy, and public education.

Those early experiences helped me understand more fully the concept of context. No illness, accident, or emotional trauma ever happens in isolation. There is always a bigger picture: a family, a community, and a set of circumstances that force a person to seek medical attention. In retrospect, I realize that it was the relationship between my patients' experiences, emotionally and physically, and the larger environment around their experience, which interested me.

This underlying theme led me to pursue a variety of interests and activities, where I could explore the relationship between what we see and experience at the personal, more local level, and the contributing factors at the systemic, global level. This interest pulled me forward into politics and the production of an educational series for public television, and it was the reason for my eventual move to Washington, DC. It pushed me to pursue more education, a variety of apprenticeships, as well as new people and projects. It allowed me to expand my thinking, interests, and expertise into business, economics, and international affairs. And ultimately, it led me back to science.

Mine has been an interesting and complex journey. But somehow it has all worked together to create the personal context, which allowed the details of the new science and its potential applications to the larger sociopolitical world to capture and hold my attention for almost a decade.

After experimenting with the applications of chaos theory for a few years, I finally felt ready to put my thoughts on paper. In the winter of 1992–93 I wrote my first paper on the subject, "Chaos: A Context for Strategic Thinking." I gave it to several friends, who thought I was onto something. So, in the summer of 1993, I offered to conduct an afternoon workshop for the World Future Society, during its Seventh General Assembly and Exposition, which was being held at the Sheraton Hotel in Washington, DC.

I was assigned to a room that would seat fifty people, but almost three hundred showed up! The conference coordinator saw what was happening in the hallway outside my room. He interrupted my opening remarks in order to move the session to a ballroom. I was overwhelmed by the response, but managed to get through the session without my slides or other visuals, which were useless in such a big room. The audio tape from my session was that year's best-seller.

The conference planning committee invited me back the next year. For the 1994 conference, held in Boston, I conducted two sessions under the expanded title, "Chaos, Complexity & Change: A Context for Strategic Thinking." And I used a new multi-media presentation, which Walter LaMendola and I developed specifically for that conference. By then I had realized that the topic was so complex that it needed to be presented in a visual format, and Walter offered to shepherd my use of this new technology. He also understood that a visual presentation supported one of the central tenets of my work: *Visual thinking is the key to strategic thinking.*

While the audience was intrigued by the integration of video, still photography, music, and original animation, I felt that I needed to go back to the drawing board. Although the feedback was generally very good, I realized that I still had to make a tighter connection between the actual science, my applications, and the use of visual information to communicate my ideas. Nevertheless, audio tapes from both sessions were among the top sixteen best-sellers for that conference.

A few weeks before the Boston conference, I received a call from Janet Coleman, who became my first editor for this book. Janet and I traveled a long and interesting road together, which eventually led both of us to The Free Press at Simon & Schuster. She nurtured this book from its beginning, eventually leaving it in the very capable hands of Liz Maguire and Stephen Morrow, in the summer of 1997, when she accepted an exciting career opportunity and moved to another publishing house.

During this same time frame, I was introduced by a friend to Lawrence Hudetz, a photographer living in Oregon, who had been using concepts from the new science in his photographic work for several years. We eventually decided to put together a workshop using photography to introduce key concepts from the new science and as an introduction to my presentation on the applications.

Working with Larry always requires that we find a beautiful location, and we have been fortunate to work together in Oregon and at Esalen Institute in Big Sur, California. Integrating our approaches and working with trusting souls from a variety of backgrounds has been a wonderful creative experience, one that greatly enriched the process of writing this book.

A Closing Comment

As you can tell from this short background story, the book you are about to read has been a work in progress for almost a decade. Over the years, the concepts, principles, and tools described in the following pages have been tried, tested, and refined successfully with individuals, businesses of all types and sizes, and with a variety of government agencies and nonprofit organizations. I feel confident that you will find them easy to use in your own organization.

So, go with me on this journey, but remember that we are all modern-day explorers. Just as the new science continues to evolve, so will our thinking about its applications. In a sense, we are painting at the edge of the map. Together, we'll continue to open and settle this exciting new territory, and I look forward to meeting you along the way.

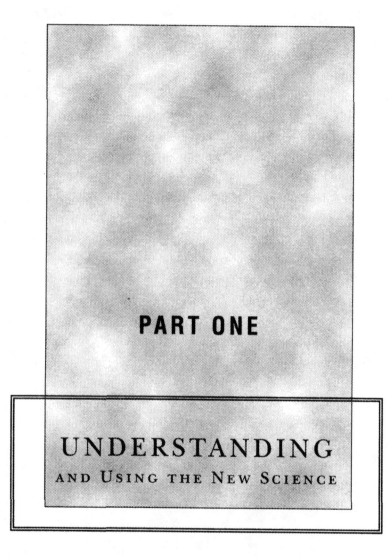

PART ONE

UNDERSTANDING
AND USING THE NEW SCIENCE

LISTEN TO THE FOOTPRINTS

You must first be on the path, before you can turn and walk into the wild.

—GARY SNYDER

The Practice of the Wild

Imagine what it would be like if every day were just like the day before. Only one season, spring. Trees and flowers in full bloom. Children, the same children, play in the park; no births, no deaths. Politicians give the same speeches over and over. No new wrinkles, gray hair, or bulges at the waistline. The sweetness of spring fills the air and our hearts are open to all possibilities. Only there aren't any. In a world of sameness, the only possibility is that somehow something might change.

Now imagine this same scene set in motion. Children grow up, we begin to see the signs of aging, and we and our loved ones leave each other by choice or by death. Conflicts arise. Businesses expand and contract. The sweetness of spring becomes the fullness of summer. Our hearts feel the ups and downs of all our experiences, and we realize that in a world of change the possibilities are endless.

. . .

Every culture since the dawn of humankind has faced the challenge of explaining *why* and *how* things change. Where do stars come from? What causes the sun to push the stars aside and fill the morning sky with light? Why does a full moon gradually shrink into a crescent? Why do volcanoes erupt? Why was one tribe victorious over another? How do new tools come into existence? Where do new ideas come from? What causes disease? We live in a world of constant change, and the explanations about it are as varied and interesting as the cultures they reflect. In looking back, history reveals that the answers to these types of questions were shaped by the underlying worldview of each culture.

For the earliest cultures it was observation and imagination, which grew into rich mythologies. The Greeks used a combination of mythology, philosophy, and science. Later, Christianity, Judaism, and Islam provided religious explanations. And now, modern science and its primary language, mathematics, are the dominant sources of our worldview.

It's misleading to think that science can be understood in isolation from the social, cultural, and political contexts in which it developed. It's even more misleading to think of science as a timeline, the kind we all memorized in school; a straight line of names and dates attributed to specific events, discoveries, and theories. But it is important to understand how science has and continues to influence our view of the world.

I prefer to think of the history of science as a collection of campfires—*campfires of thought*—dotting the social, cultural and political fields of their time. Imagine that each campfire represents the *conceptual* essence of those gathered around it. In order to appreciate the connections and relationships among these conceptual clusters, as well as their contributions to generations of future thinkers, we need an aerial view.

From above, we see that some fires (*ideas*) burn brightly for a while and then go out; others never quite catch on; some become wildfires as they consume those nearby; in some places, sparks from existing fires ignite new ones; a few burn eternally; occasionally, twin fires burn like pillars of light until one grows stronger or the ground between them catches fire, creating a single column of light; some die down, then catch a gust of wind, flare up, and burn for a while longer; and others glow softly in the background, their embers keeping ancient memories alive.

The history of science is a relatively new discipline, and as such there is still much to learn about the contributions of early cultures to the evolution of science. With that caveat in mind, the campfire image helps us appreciate the fact that there is an historical field or context in which new ideas develop. It helps us recognize the similarities as well as the diversity of thinking that developed in different parts of the world during the same time period. And it helps us appreciate the important impact that contact with other cultures and other schools of thought have on the spread and evolution of new ideas.

Historians usually have a purpose or an agenda. In my case, it's to follow the theme of change from the scientific perspective, which I believe will help us understand some of our present-day dilemmas. By listening to the voices of those who came before us we'll understand how we developed our preference for linear, mechanistic thinking and the assumptions by which we live and work. And we'll begin to understand the limitations of this worldview.

Beginning with a scientific retrospective will also help us understand the context in which the new science of chaos theory and complexity began to take shape, and why it is generating so much excitement. In that light, I invite you to ride with me through the fields of history visiting briefly the major *campfires of thought* leading to the present.

Our view of history is rarely complete. New discoveries often surprise us by pointing to much earlier and higher levels of knowledge and skill than current theories suggest. For example, we now know that by the time Egyptian civilization made the transition to hieroglyphic writing its science, art, astrology, astronomy, and architecture were all well-developed.[1]

The span of human *pre*history is enormous, covering the million or more years preceding the development of the first written languages, which appeared around B.C. 3000.[2] Archaeological evidence is often fragmented, separated by continents, still buried, or destroyed by cataclysmic events or dramatic changes in the Earth's climate. Because of this, little is actually known about the worldview of those who lived before the time of written history.

However, by studying the earliest written records, artifacts, and the stories that exist in oral traditions today, anthropologists and historians have found clues to the belief systems of those who lived just before and after the beginnings of recorded history. These early cultures saw the world as an interconnected whole in which man, nature, a variety of mythological characters, and many types of invisible forces worked together to bring the world into its present form.[3]

Each culture had an elaborate creation story and a collection of other stories that explained the natural, social, and technical changes leading to the present. In these prereligious cultures the gods were an immanent part of the universe, not transcendent as religious leaders would later proclaim. And as such, the deities played an active role in human affairs, and nature's extremes were seen as expressions of divine anger or benevolence toward humankind.

Inconsistencies and contradictions were irrelevant as long as the stories satisfied questions about the past and supported stability in the present.[4] For example, the origins of the world, its peoples, plants, and animals usually are attributed to the sexual activity and progeny of various gods and goddesses.

The gods often fought among themselves. Even when killed and dismembered, a hero's body could be reassembled long enough to accomplish an important task. And to account for new tools or insights, stories were expanded to include the hero's use of the new "whatever" in his victory.

In Western culture, we are accustomed to thinking of myth as merely fiction. But when viewed from the perspective of psychology, for example, rather than from those of anthropology or history, we see contemporary personal and interpersonal themes enacted in the mythological dramas—love, betrayal, death, the struggle for power, and the search for wisdom. These universal or archetypal themes help explain the renaissance of mythology as demonstrated in the work of Carl Jung, Joseph Campbell, Robert Bly, Jean Shinoda Bolen, and Clarissa Pinkola Estés.

Myths accounted for the mundane as well as the extraordinary, and in doing so they also represent the earliest cosmologies or beliefs about how the world works as a whole. There are a variety of stories telling how the world was formed out of its primordial elements. Each culture had its own version and specific names for the gods and goddesses who gave form to the formless.

What most of the stories have in common is a description of the universe as a *dynamic* or constantly changing field of vital substances out of which the gods created life and all its forms. In the content of these ancient cosmologies, we catch glimpses of the conceptual gene pool from which scientific thought began to evolve.

In the sixth and fifth centuries B.C., Greece became the first culture in which literacy played a crucial role. Writing allowed ideas and information to be stored, transferred, compared, supplemented, and critiqued. This accomplishment, along with the Greek skill of borrowing and integrating ideas from other cultures, laid the foundation for its spectacular achievements in many areas, but especially in philosophy and science.

The Greeks borrowed mathematics from Egypt and Mesopotamia, now southern Iraq, where Pythagoras was said to have traveled in the fifth century B.C. From these same cultures they also borrowed developments in astronomy, pharmacology, and surgery. And its geographic location and trade routes provided contact with Eastern cultures and traditions.

Philosophy and science began to emerge in the midst of this culture steeped in its own mythology and a mythologically based cosmology. Stories about Zeus and the other gods of Mount Olympus were a central part of Greek life, and they continued to be long after the development of a new, more intellectual approach to understanding the world.

The word "philosophy" is a broad term with roots in both the Greek *philosophos* and the Latin *philosophia,* meaning love of wisdom. To take a philosophical approach to any subject means to prefer the methods of intellect and logic over experience and intuition. The early Greek philosophers developed this approach by first applying it to questions about nature and later to questions about politics, ethics, and a number of other subjects.

The more specific word "science," derived from the Greek word *episteme,* or epistemology, and the Latin word *scientia,* means knowledge gained through careful and deliberate methodologies. Together, the closely related concepts of philosophy and science represent the *cultivation of knowledge through reasoning, experimentation, critique, and proof.*

The word "scientist" first appeared in 1840.[5] Until then, the person we would now call a scientist was identified by using the word "philosopher" hyphenated with the specific scientific discipline in which the individual worked, resulting in descriptors such as philosopher-mathematician and philosopher-geographer.

In the sixth century B.C., ancient Greece covered a much larger territory than the Greece we know today, and these early philosophical developments emerged in its easternmost region or present-day Turkey. In this region, separated from the Greek mainland by the Aegean Sea, a group of innovative thinkers began a careful, more exacting or philosophical inquiry into the process of change.

"Natural philosophy" or the "philosophy of nature" began to take shape as this group of radical sixth-century Greek thinkers started asking new questions about how one thing comes into existence and another is transformed. They wanted to understand what the world is made of: what are its ingredients? how do they interact? They tried to understand the basic nature, characteristics, or principles at work in the world around them.

They believed that all things work or change according to their basic natures. A volcano erupts in a certain way because that's what volcanoes do. The moon and stars move according to their natures. In other words, order was intrinsic. If everything behaves according to its nature, then the world is orderly and predictable. And the challenge, as they saw it, was to understand the basic nature of specific phenomena and to determine if generalizations or broad principles applied across phenomena.

With this type of thinking, this group of philosophers and their followers made three important contributions toward the development of the scientific method. First, they asked new types of questions designed to help them understand the fundamental nature of the universe. What is the relationship between order and change? What exists before form? Is there a common "something" out of which all forms are created? If so, what is it? What are its characteristics? And what happens to it at death?

Second, their answers eliminated the gods as the probable cause of natural phenomena. The belief in a world unpredictable and vulnerable at the hands of the gods was replaced by the belief in a more orderly and predictable world that could be understood by understanding its fundamental realities.

And third, they began to develop a formal system of scientific inquiry. Theorists were expected to provide proof of the correctness of their ideas for review and critique. In other words, the quest for truth and the development of criteria by which to recognize it had begun.

This type of thinking did not follow a straight line to the present. Like an epic mystery, the history of science is filled with false starts, dead ends, new clues, hidden passageways, startling discoveries, and a cast of characters to keep the story moving.

Many schools of thought followed. The atomists in the late fifth century B.C. believed that the world was made up of tiny constantly moving particles, which came in a variety of shapes and sizes and out of which everything in the material world was constructed. In their view, life and all its forms are made up of these lifeless particles and life itself is a well-constructed machine. This mechanistic view of the world would fade under the influence of Plato and Aristotle, only to reappear stronger than ever in the seventeenth century.

Pythagorean philosophy, emanating from the Greek colonies of southern Italy, introduced the idea that fundamental reality is numerical, not material. For Pythagoreans, numbers came first, then matter. Mathematics was their tool of choice for investigating the world.

Questions about the nature of the world and the processes of change provoked questions about the reality of change. Shouldn't ultimate reality by definition be unchangeable? And if so, how could something unchangeable produce change? The possibility of such a paradox—a world that is both stable and changeable—sparked new theoretical conflicts between the concept of *being* and that of *becoming*.

Heraclitus, who is credited with the saying that "it's impossible to step into the same river twice," believed that the universe is characterized by constant change. He argued that order or equilibrium results from the tension between opposing forces.

Parmenides, who denied the existence of time, took the opposite view. Change is not possible. What exists now has always existed. From his perspective, even the experience of change must be overlooked in favor of a rational approach to reality.

Others took compromise positions. Change and stability coexist. An underlying stability is present beneath our superficial experience of change.

Another feature of these early debates were the ongoing questions about the role of the *elements:* fire, water, air, earth; the *senses:* color, taste, odor, sound, texture; and *values* such as good, evil, honor, justice, etc. Was fire the original material of the universe? If the gods created

and guided the universe, what were their intentions? And, of what bene-
fit were the senses in understanding fundamental reality?

In the fourth century B.C., Socrates shifted the focus of philosophy away
from cosmology and toward politics and ethics. But his disciple, Plato,
influenced by his teacher and the Pythagoreans, continued to explore
the underlying basis of reality.

Plato envisioned two realms: a superior changeless realm of ideas and
forms; and the ever-changing material world, an imperfect expression
of this higher realm. Because the material world is transitory, he
believed that true reality exists only in the realm of ideas and forms.
Therefore, the world we see and experience through our senses is but a
shadow of the true reality. To know the true reality, we must be freed
from the senses. He believed that the senses are useful, but that the path
to knowledge is reason.

How did Plato's approach relate to the thinking of his predecessors?
First, rather than a fiery cosmos, he believed in a realm of forms and
ideas from which everything in the material world was derived. Second,
he accounted for both change and stability by assigning them to different realms. Third, he placed the senses in opposition to reason. And
finally, he believed that everything in the material world was a representation, although imperfect, of its perfect form in the higher realm.
Because of this, careful observation of the material world would provide
insights about the true nature of the universe.

Plato disagreed with the earlier philosophical views, which attributed
order to the inherent or intrinsic nature of things. This view of order, he
said, excluded any divine plan for the universe.

To explain his thinking, he used the image of a divine craftsman-
mathematician who imposed order from the outside by using geometric principles to construct the universe. In what appears to us like a leap
of imagination, he believed that each element—fire, air, and water—
could be translated into a geometric shape based on the triangle, the

tetrahedron, the octahedron, and the icosahedron respectively. He used the cube to represent earth and the dodecahedron, made of twelve pentagons and resembling an angular sphere, to represent the universe as a whole.

In his view, creation was the result of various combinations of triangles. We would be tempted to say, "various combinations of these *triangular* elements," but Plato believed that triangles were the fundamental reality out of which everything is made. Here you can see how Plato's cosmology derives from his belief in the ultimate reality of shape and form. Change and diversity occurred through various combinations and recombinations of triangles.

On the surface, Plato's cosmology appears somewhat mechanistic. But the difference between his view and that of the atomists, who believed that the universal substance was lifeless, is that he also believed that the creator-craftsman created a living universe with a soul, which is responsible for its well-being.

It's helpful to remember that Plato believed that man and all material objects are imperfect replicas of the perfect world of shape and form. So, if man has a soul, then the universe is a more perfect being with a more perfect soul. His was an animated universe, a living geometrically perfect cosmos.

He also believed that the universe is supported by various noninterfering gods whose role is to ensure stability and order. In other words, he restored the gods to account for order, the very reason that the earlier philosophers had removed them. And by using geometry to describe the world, he was a proponent of reducing nature to numbers.

Through Plato's work and the work of those who came before him, we see the struggle to create a conceptual framework within which to understand a world characterized by both order and change. Plato's worldview dominated the thinking of his time, but Aristotle (born in 384 B.C.), Plato's student, disagreed with many of his teacher's beliefs and set in motion another worldview, which would dominate philosophical and scientific thought for almost two thousand years.

. . .

Aristotle's greatest achievement was that he developed a formal system of logic and a set of principles, which he applied to a wide range of disciplines, including biology, cosmology, meteorology, astronomy, and what would later be called theology. His interests were broad and his thinking complex, thus accounting for his influence across so many generations.

Aristotle did not accept Plato's view that the senses are stumbling blocks to knowledge; nor did he believe that the material world is an imperfect representation of a more perfect external reality. In his view, the material world is reality, and knowledge of it begins with experience and experience begins with the senses.

Like the earlier philosophers, Aristotle believed that natural objects, as opposed to man-made objects, behave in certain ways according to their natures. He believed that through observation and experience (empirical knowledge) and the use of inductive and deductive reasoning one could understand the basic nature of things. He believed that all objects are made of both form and matter. But unlike Plato, who believed that form is foremost and separate from matter, Aristotle believed that they are inseparable.

For Aristotle, the word "form" meant not only shape, but included other characteristics or qualities such as color, texture, and temperature. And matter is the substance through which these qualities become recognizable. Qualities do not exist without matter, and matter is differentiated by its qualities.

Therefore, Aristotle's world was primarily qualitative rather than quantitative, as distinguished from the mathematical worldview preferred by Plato and the Pythagoreans. This helps explain why he favored observation and description over experimentation.

Aristotle believed that the form an object takes is determined by its function. To understand the shape of a foot, for example, we would have to understand the function of feet: weight-bearing, balance, and locomotion.

He also believed that, while form may change, matter remains. Change is possible, he said, because matter contains the potential for change. For example, a tulip bulb contains the potential for becoming a tulip. The characteristics or qualities of the tulip change as it fulfills (grows into) its potential, which it does according to its individual nature as well as the general nature of tulips as differentiated from other types of flowers.

He believed that the material world is changing constantly because every object is in the process of becoming what it is intended to become, a type of self-actualizing process. In other words, change occurs as objects move toward their final outcomes according to their natures.

Aristotle's accomplishments were enormous. His views dominated the philosophical and scientific thinking of many disciplines for almost two millennia, and endure even today. Yet, it is his cosmology, or rather Galileo's break with it in the seventeenth century, for which he is most often remembered.

Aristotle believed that the universe was eternal; no beginning, no end. He believed that the Earth was round rather than flat, but he also believed that the Earth was the center of the universe, with the sun, moon, stars, and planets revolving around it in perfect circular orbits. He imagined that the universe itself was a giant sphere divided into two realms, terrestrial and celestial. The Earth, and the region between the earth and the moon, made up the terrestrial realm. Everything above the moon was in the celestial realm. Each realm operated according to a different set of principles.

The terrestrial realm, made out of the four elements—earth, air, fire, and water—was subject to the principles of form and matter and, therefore, characterized by constant change. The celestial realm, by contrast, was made of a perfect and unchanging fifth element, which Aristotle called "aether." (Aether is the poetic name for the clear upper air breathed by Zeus and the other gods of Mount Olympus in Greek mythology.) According to Aristotle, everything in the celestial realm was perfect and followed perfect unchanging cycles.

Motion in the celestial region was not the same kind of motion experienced in the terrestrial region. According to Aristotle, the Earth and all objects in the terrestrial realm were stationary except when seeking their natural place in the universe (natural motion) or when forced to move (forced motion).

He believed that an object that has been forced or caused to move eventually would resume a resting state, until forced to move again. Resistance was also a factor in forced motion, influencing both time and distance. And because Earth was at the center of the universe, each object moved toward its natural place in relationship to that center. Motion in the terrestrial realm was rectilinear and characterized by breaks and interruptions.

In the celestial realm, things were different. He believed that motion in the celestial realm was not forced but inspired by the perfection of a supreme and changeless diety whom he called the "Prime Mover."

He believed that celestial motion followed his theory of function, or final outcome. According to Aristotle, the sphere and its counterpart, the circle, represented perfection. Therefore, the heavenly bodies, assigned to a series of concentric spheres, moved in perfect continuous unchanging circular orbits, because they were attempting to fulfill their potentials. Because perfection was the final outcome for heavenly bodies, he believed that perfect and continuous circular motion was the only type of motion found in the celestial realm.

If we could animate Aristotle's view of the universe, what would it look like? Imagine that you are in a hot air balloon hovering above a baseball stadium on a clear summer night. Below, you see a game in progress with players on the field and one at bat. The pitcher throws the ball, you hear the crack of the bat as the batter swings, and the ball goes flying through the air. In the stands you see the fans jumping up and down, shouting at the players, talking to each other, and eating. And you hear the roar of the crowd as a player slides into home plate.

You are also aware that surrounding the stadium are the night lights, activities, and sounds of a bustling metropolitan area. And in the distance you see a shooting star streaking across the horizon. From the balloon, you observe all types of forced and discontinuous terrestrial activity.

Now, look up at the sky. Above the sights and sounds of the city below, you see the moon. And beyond the moon, you see the celestial realm with distant stars and planets rotating around the Earth in perfect circular orbits. Now, close your eyes, take a deep breath, and imagine the sense of comfort you would feel in believing that the Earth is the center of the universe, sheltered beneath a canopy of unchanging heavenly perfection.

Aristotle's cosmology was quite complex. It was modified in the second century by Ptolemy, who developed a whole cosmological model, which served as the basis for elaborate celestial maps. The Aristotelian-Ptolemaic cosmos was based more on conceptualization than on observation and experimentation, which would be its downfall centuries later. The move away from the Aristotelian worldview is often cited as the point of demarcation between medieval science and the beginning of modern science, ushered in by the Scientific Revolution of the seventeenth century.

From these *campfires of thought,* we can identify the major philosophical and scientific questions, and the poles around which the answers revolved. *What is the fundamental nature of reality?* Lifeless atoms floating in the void of space (mechanistic) or a living material (organic), perhaps with a guiding intelligence of some sort? *What is the nature of change and its relationship to stability and order?* Intrinsic or extrinsic? *What is the best way to answer these questions?* Is it with qualitative methods such as observation and description or by applying the quantitative methods of mathematics?

In various forms these debates raged on for centuries, against the backdrop of enormous social and political change, including the expansion of the Greek empire and its eventual demise; the rise and fall of the Roman Empire; the birth and expansion of Christianity in the West and Islam in the East; relentless political upheaval in Europe; and the institution of schools and universities throughout the Western world.

Before we go back to the major questions, I want to discuss briefly several aspects of the interesting and important relationship of the Church to science. By the time of Julius Caesar's death in 44 B.C., the Roman Empire included most of Spain as well as present-day France and England. It extended down across the Mediterranean Sea into North Africa and Egypt, across Greece and the Greek territories, and into present-day Turkey. Virtually the entire Mediterranean basin was Roman territory.

The success of Rome in conquering Greece meant that Rome began to absorb the Greek intellectual traditions. Knowledge of Greek philosophy became a status symbol of the Roman upper class, thus popularizing and supporting the translation of Greek texts into Latin.

In the first century A.D., Christianity began to spread through the Roman Empire, north from Jerusalem along the coast of the Mediterranean Sea and west across present-day Turkey and Greece and into Rome. In the beginning, Christians faced resistance and contempt from Greco-Roman intellectuals and the threat of persecution from the Empire itself. Eventually, however, resistance turned to toleration, and by the end of the fourth century Christianity had become the state religion. By forming an official alliance with the Church, the Roman state hoped to strengthen its control and unify the Empire.

The early Christian communities took many forms, depending on the geographic location and culture of its earliest followers and their pre-Christian beliefs about the nature of man, god, and the universe. This created a great deal of diversity among the early churches and led to disputes about the nature and practice of Christianity.

Assisted by a succession of Roman emperors, the Latin Church eventually consolidated its power in Rome. The local church of Rome and its bishop assumed a preeminent role among the loose-knit network of churches throughout the Empire. From its center in Rome, the Church worked to resolve doctrinal disputes among local churches by developing a unified doctrine and a disciplined organization.[6]

The Church of Rome based its religious authority on the belief that it was founded by the apostle Peter, who was later martyred and buried there, and on the belief that he established a line of succession and communication through the bishop of Rome. The Petrine primacy, acknowledged today by the symbolic importance of St. Peter's Basilica in Rome, is what fundamentally distinguishes Catholicism from other forms of Christianity.

Because the masses were relatively uneducated, the intellectuals of the early Church assumed a powerful role as they worked to develop a unified Church doctrine, respond to the intellectual works of the pre-Christian Greek philosophers, and spread the teachings and mission of the Church throughout the medieval Western world. In other words, the Catholic Church, headquartered in Rome, assumed three important roles: keeper of the faith; translator of important written works, including the Bible and the Greek classics; and educator of the masses. This combination gave the Church an enormous amount of control over the thinking and belief system of its followers.

Formal education remained a privilege of the upper class through the duration of the Roman Empire. As Rome's influence began to fade, and Western civilization entered a period of social chaos, the availability of educational opportunities shrank. Christian intellectuals retreated to monasteries in which they could pursue their interests, while the rest of Western society struggled with social and political turmoil and the plagues that ravaged whole regions.

The Dark Age of scientific and intellectual pursuit (approximately A.D. 500–1000) had descended. During this time, however, some monastic traditions allowed and others even encouraged their monks to continue annotating, transcribing, and translating ancient texts while at the same time building libraries filled with their own scholarly works. In other words, monasteries provided a safe place through which many of the classics survived, while also providing a safe haven for Christian intellectualism.

During this period, medieval Western civilization was anything but civilized, as generations of warlords fought for control over each others' territories. Eventually, feudal states began to emerge out of territorial conquests, paving the way for the rise of nations. Throughout this time the Church remained the most stable institution in medieval life.

Scholarly activity and education began to reemerge during the reign of Charlemagne, whose kingdom, by the time of his death in 814, extended through Germany, France, Switzerland, and Austria, and into Italy. His educational reforms were undertaken to strengthen both the Church and the state. With this purpose in mind, education was conducted in church schools established throughout his territory.

The transition period in which learning began to spread from the monasteries into society and the Renaissance, or rebirth of intellectual pursuit, covers approximately four and one-half centuries, 1000–1450. By this time, the Catholic Church, the *de facto* heir to the Roman Empire, was the most powerful institution in medieval Europe.

During this 450-year revival, Latin and Greek texts were recovered, new texts trickled in from other parts of the world (primarily Islamic texts and their commentaries on the work of the Greek philosophers), and the Church tried to assimilate these important but nonconforming intellectual works into its doctrine.

Aristotle's work, because of its breadth and intellectual rigor, assumed a central role in the reemergence of philosophy and science. His concept of the universe, with Earth at the center, suited the Church's desire for unity and power. So, his view of the cosmos was adopted by the Church, not because of its scientific underpinnings, but because it supported the Church's view of itself at the center of society. In other words, the Church institutionalized the Aristotelian worldview. To question it was to question the Church, an act for which one could be charged with heresy.

In the twelfth century, afraid that its power was being eroded by critics, doubters, and "new thinkers," the Catholic Church established the Inquisition to ensure uniformity of religious belief in European society.[7] By punishing those who questioned its doctrine and authority, the Church hoped to maintain control over and stabilize a society, which was increasingly more mobile and open to outside influences. The

Inquisition was a powerful weapon of the Church for seven centuries, reaching its peak in the fifteenth and sixteenth centuries.

Its demise was set in motion by the Protestant Reformation, which spread across Europe in the 1500s, and by the French Revolution in 1789, which promoted freedom of religion and religious tolerance. The Inquisition continued to be used sporadically into the nineteenth century and was finally abolished by the Holy Office in Rome in 1852.

The fact of the Inquisition demonstrates clearly the power of the medieval Church and its desire to control the behavior and thinking of millions. Individuals engaged in any type of activity that threatened to undermine the Church's authority, including those exploring new scientific ideas, were subject to its tortures.

In the seventeenth century, Galileo, the "father of modern science," was threatened with torture for promoting the Copernican theory that the Earth revolves around the Sun, contrary to the accepted Aristotelian theory that the Earth was the center of the universe. He was forced by the Church to renounce his own views. In the end Galileo's views were accepted, but he was not absolved as a heretic until 1984, over three hundred and fifty years later!

The struggle between science and religion to understand and unravel their relationship has been long and complicated, and extends into the present. The contemporary argument over educational curricula, between those who support creationism, or a literal interpretation of the Bible's seven-day creation story, and those who accept the theory of evolution is a modern-day version of this historic dilemma.

The Scientific Revolution of the seventeenth century was not an event but rather a period of transition in which open questions from the past were resolved and revolutionary new ideas began to take hold. Some *campfires of thought* were extinguished forever, while others were ignited and still light the scientific landscape today.

In his essay "Statistical Expectations," Daniel Boorstin writes, "The whole advance from ancient to modern science has often been summed up as a movement from qualities to quantities."[8] Indeed, by the time the seventeenth century arrived two separate but converging movements were already underway—the mathematization of nature and the development of a mechanical philosophy—which would eventually replace Aristotle's natural philosophy.

While there were many who contributed to this revolution in thinking, it was the works of Johannes Kepler, Galileo Galilei, René Descartes, Christiaan Huygens, and Sir Isaac Newton that dominated and completed the transition from medieval science to modern science. And two new instruments of observation, the telescope and the microscope, gave scientists the tools they needed to push their thinking forward.

The intellectual milieu of seventeenth-century Europe was diverse and volatile. Tension between Protestants and Catholics; an increase in the availability of printed texts; a growing number of educated people; an increase in the number of individuals studying philosophy, science, and theology; and, the expansion of knowledge through stories and objects brought back to Europe by travelers and explorers created fertile ground for new ideas. It was as if the ground heaved occasionally from the lava flow of creative tension just below the surface.

Eventually, new ideas began to break through, and the ensuing eruption was dramatic enough, even at the time, to look like a complete break with the past. But the seeds of this revolution, like all others, were sown in a field of growing discontent. The old answers did not respond adequately to new information and new questions. So, it was precisely this tension between the old and the new that gave form and substance to the rapid advances that took place in this time period.

While Aristotle believed that mathematics had an important place in science, he believed that there was a difference between mathematics and the reality of the changeable world he wanted to understand. Plato and the Pythagoreans, on the other hand, believed that nature was constructed according to geometric principles and therefore required a mathematical approach to understanding. So, while Aristotle's cosmology provided an overarching conceptual framework for thinking about the universe as a whole, the Platonic-Pythagorean approach evolved in parallel as a way to describe the invisible principles at work behind visible phenomena.

By the end of the seventeenth century, Aristotle's natural philosophy had been replaced by mechanical philosophy, which viewed nature as a huge machine whose underlying mechanisms could be understood and explained. Eventually, mechanistic thinking converged with the Platonic-Pythagorean approach to form a mechanistic-mathematical view of nature, epitomized by the metaphor of a "clockwork" universe.

This transition was set in motion before the end of the sixteenth century by Nicolaus Copernicus, a Polish priest, who theorized that the Sun, not the Earth, was the center of the universe. Copernicus' work was published in 1543, but it went relatively unnoticed for over fifty years, until Galileo Galilei, an Italian astronomer, and his German contemporary, Johannes Kepler, undertook the challenge of confirming the truth of the Copernican system. It's unlikely that they ever met, and in many ways their views were contradictory. Nevertheless, they were kindred spirits and together their work completed the revolution in astronomical theory started by Copernicus.

In the Copernican system, not only was the Earth not the center of the universe, but neither was it stationary. The Earth had two motions: a daily rotation around its own axis and an annual rotation around the Sun. This radical proposition raised a whole set of new questions about motion in the heavens.

In the second half of the sixteenth century, astronomers observed a new star and a comet that appeared to be in the region beyond the moon, the celestial region, which was thought to be unchanging. This, along with Copernicus' theories, convinced Kepler that Aristotle's celestial spheres did not exist and that other explanations must be found for planetary motion. He devoted his career to developing new theories to explain *celestial* motion.

Like Copernicus, Kepler believed that the universe is constructed according to geometric principles, and his work reflected his desire to provide proof of its geometric structure, while at the same time uncovering the physical causes behind observable phenomena. Kepler was the first to propose that the same set of mechanical principles applied to both the celestial and terrestrial realms. He eventually proved that the orbits of planets are ellipses, not circles.

He demonstrated that the planetary system does have a geometric structure. And he posed new questions about the type of forces that hold the planetary system together and cause the rotation of planets around the Sun. In other words, he shifted and expanded the theoretical framework of astronomy.

His theories were dramatic and unsettling, even to him. By supporting Copernicus' theory of a heliocentric or Sun-centered universe and by rejecting the concept of celestial spheres, Kepler shattered, at least theoretically, the view of the universe that had been accepted without question for two thousand years. But it was Galileo who provided proof of the correctness of these new ideas and drove the final wedge between the Aristotelian worldview and the thinking that would replace it.

Beginning in 1609, observations with his new telescope convinced Galileo that not only was the Sun the center of the universe, but that it was imperfect and changeable, much like objects in the terrestrial realm. This led him to question the accepted belief in two sets of rules, one for the celestial realm and another for the terrestrial realm. He too proposed that both operated according to one set of principles.

But unlike Kepler, who focused on understanding celestial motion, Galileo focused on *terrestrial* motion. Without an explanation of how the Earth could be spinning while we are standing still, this new view of the universe, which violated common sense, would never be accepted.

Galileo's explanation had two major components: the concept of inertia, that an object set in motion will continue to move with uniform velocity until something acts to stop it; and the separation of motion from the Aristotelian idea of essential natures. In developing his theory of motion, Galileo proposed a whole new mechanics to explain it.

According to Galileo, objects are indifferent to motion. On a rotating Earth, motion is an object's natural state. The motion of the Earth's rotation is not obvious because it is an experience shared by all. It does not act independently on any object, but uniformly on all objects. All objects experience a uniform horizontal movement, which relates to the Earth's circular rotation. It is eternal and imperceptible.

Think about an airplane ride. Everyone and everything on the plane move in the same direction at the same time and speed. On a clear day, only the sound of the plane or a look out the window give you a sense of motion. You are much more aware of your individual movements and the movements of other passengers than you are of the plane's motion, unless of course it runs into local air turbulence. In other words, according to Galileo, a hat stays on your head because it shares the same unvarying motion as all objects on Earth. Only *local* motion or a change in geographic location is perceptible and requires an explanation.

Objects are passive, and a change in location (local motion) is caused by external forces, not internal causes, essential natures, or unique qualities, as described by Aristotle. By focusing only on local motion and by separating motion from essential natures, Galileo shifted the study of motion from *causes* to *forces,* and by doing so dismissed a large part of Aristotle's natural philosophy.

Galileo, like many others, believed in the importance of mathematical reasoning and used geometric ratios to express his theory of motion in terms of velocity, acceleration, time, and distance. So, in stripping away the qualities that Aristotle enjoyed exploring in favor of the quantities that remained, Galileo was able to make his greatest contribution to modern science: mathematizing the study of motion.

With his theory of motion, Galileo succeeded in answering the major objections to the Copernican heliocentric universe. Public acceptance was still slow, but without Galileo's work it would never have been possible. His work not only laid the foundation for acceptance, but it also established the basic physical principles and questions on which modern science is based.

The deconstruction of the Aristotelian worldview paved the way for other dramatic changes. However, only in retrospect do these changes seem to create a coherent and direct path to the present. In fact, many modern historians reject this artificial sense of coherence, preferring instead to examine the various threads, themes, or *campfires of thought* that contributed to the shift in thinking known as the Scientific Revolution.

For our purposes, it's the outcomes of this historic period and their impact on our thinking that are important. Therefore, the following summary is organized according to themes, with references to individuals or groups of individuals who made important contributions.

The Mechanical Philosophy

In Aristotle's natural philosophy, change was the result of a self-actualizing or becoming process through which natural objects fulfilled their potentials. An acorn becomes an oak tree and a tadpole grows into a frog, each according to its nature. Aristotle believed that one could understand the basic nature of things by observing and describing this process. His was an orderly, dynamic, and purposeful world in which nature played an active role.

Over the centuries other forms of natural philosophy appeared. In the sixteenth century, Renaissance Naturalism was a popular school of thought, in which nature was believed to possess a living spirit filled with mysteries unknowable to man's intellect. To its practitioners, the magnet, with its mysterious powers of attraction, was an example of nature's occult forces and hidden powers.

Although different in many ways, Aristotelian natural philosophy and Renaissance Naturalism shared a belief in nature's *active* participation in the world through the interconnectedness of mind, matter, and spirit. However, opposition to this view of nature began to grow, reaching its peak in the seventeenth century, and René Descartes was its most influential critic.

While Kepler and Galileo both used mechanical explanations to describe the Copernican universe, the move toward an organized mechanical philosophy appears to have been a spontaneous reaction against animism and the attribution of humanlike qualities to nature, which according to its opponents contributed little to science and its understanding of the world. For Descartes and others, the machine metaphor was a much more powerful tool for understanding nature.

Although no one can totally escape the influence of the past, in his mind at least, Descartes made a clean start. The cornerstone of Cartesian mechanism was the separation of mind from matter. In taking this dualistic approach, Descartes expunged every trace of intelligence and life from nature, viewing it instead as *passive* lifeless matter to be acted upon by outside forces. He believed that all matter, including the human body, operates like a machine with mechanisms that are understandable by the mind's rational intellect.

In separating mind from matter, Decartes depersonalized knowledge, thereby creating a chasm between one's experience of reality and reality as interpreted by science. He separated objective reality from the subjective experience of reality.

Descartes did not attempt to develop new theories for natural phenomena. Instead, he devised new explanations or interpretations for known phenomena, using mechanical descriptions. In his book *The Construction of Modern Science,* Richard Westfall describes Descartes' approach succinctly: "Earlier philosophies had seen nature in organic terms. Descartes turned the tables by picturing even organic phenomena as mechanisms."[9]

The clock, because of its central place in European society, became the metaphor of choice for explaining the mechanics at work behind the visible world. The shift from natural time, based on seasonal rhythms and the Sun, to mechanical time, divided into equal hours and minutes, was hailed as an enormous technological accomplishment. Today tourists are still charmed by the old elaborately designed clocks and clock towers found throughout Europe. But this shift, from natural to man-made time, unwittingly gave the clock *machine* control over our thinking about and experience of time. Nevertheless, it was seen as an example of man's ingenuity and his ability to understand and harness nature.

So, the clock, with its uniform motions and occasional irregularities, became the perfect metaphor for nature. By the sixteenth century, it was common to find the inner workings of a clock housed behind its face and other exterior time-telling features. Thus, the hidden clock-works represented nature's hidden mechanisms. And the visible movements of the clock, which often appeared animated and intelligent, represented nature's inanimate extension of its mechanical parts working together.

In his book *The Scientific Revolution,* Steven Shapin describes the clockwork metaphor: "There might be an intelligent agent in the universe standing in the same relation to nature as clockmakers to their clocks, but one was not to confuse the inanimate product of intelligence with intelligence itself."[10] Just as a clockmaker assembles the parts of a clock to complete his overall design, so are nature's parts assembled into a complex inanimate design.

The mechanical philosophy became irresistible in its simplicity and apparent ability to explain complex phenomena. The body was described as a human machine with the heart as its central pump. The universe was described as a vortex with centrifugal forces and counter-pressures. And according to Descartes, magnetism resulted from the movement of screw-shaped particles through the Earth's core.

Mechanical philosophers also attempted to answer the question "What is matter made of?" Descartes believed that all matter was made out of three basic elements—fire, air, and earth—configured into different sizes and shapes. According to Descartes, all of nature could arise from various combinations of these three basic elements. Others believed that the universe was made up of tiny particles of various sizes, known as corpuscles, which arranged themselves into clusters to create different types of matter. Atomists believed that tiny, invisible, indivisible bits of matter were the basic material out of which everything was made.

In 1905, Einstein's description of Brownian motion—the irregular, random motion of fine particles of dust suspended in a liquid—helped to decide the debate in favor of the atomists.[11] But now we know that atoms are made up of even smaller particles. So, what are the basic building blocks of nature? At the time of this writing, scientists believe the answer is *quarks!*

Many modern-day business practices are still based on this mechanistic, building-block approach. In the early days of Total Quality Management, fishbone diagrams filled whole walls as organizations tried to identify and understand their dysfunctional parts. And today, reengineering teams examine even the smallest details of a business's operations, hoping to streamline and cut costs at every turn.

It's not that these efforts aren't useful. The problem is that too often they are disconnected from the context, dynamics, and overall direction of the organization. Recently, a senior executive with a large metropolitan health care system told me, "At the moment, we have four reengineering teams working in our system and I don't know that we can ask our managers to start a strategic planning effort in the middle of reengineering." My response was to ask, "Then how do you know whether or not you're reengineering the functions that are most central to your future success?"

In addition to being disconnected from its strategic directions, a focus on the pathology of its parts may lead an organization to overtreat a perceived illness at the expense of its future energy needs and potential. Shortsighted downsizing may immediately strengthen an organization's bottom line, while at the same time reducing its ability to respond effectively to sudden changes, crises, or unexpected opportunities. In other words, a mechanistic approach may be debilitating, futile, or even deadly without a strong connection to the big picture.

THE MATHEMATIZATION OF NATURE

The Platonic-Pythagorean tradition, dating from the fourth century B.C., promoted the belief that the universe is constructed according to mathematical principles. This belief—that mathematics would be the key to understanding and expressing the underlying structure of the universe—influenced the thinking of philosophers for centuries.

In the seventeenth century, the popularity of this approach paralleled the development of mechanical philosophy, and you can see attempts by Kepler, Galileo, and others to describe the mechanics of motion in mathematical terms. Add this to Descartes' emphasis on matter as distinct from mind, and you have the framework of seventeenth-century science: the study of matter and motion or, more accurately, the study of *matter in motion,* and the search for nature's hidden order. These two interests did not always fit together easily.

Few doubted that nature could be studied mathematically. But because a mathematical description is always an idealized account of natural phenomena, the more pressing questions concerned its accuracy and the propriety of using it to capture nature's realities and complexities. Was the creator a mathematician or was there a middle ground between the utility of mathematics and the uniqueness of the real world?

The idea that nature could be studied mathematically gave confidence to its proponents, who eventually won the debate. Many, including Dutch scientist Christiaan Huygens and English mathematician Sir

Isaac Newton, worked to perfect the mechanics and mathematics of motion. In his work *Philosophiae Naturalis Principia Mathematica* (*The Mathematical Principles of Natural Philosophy*), published in 1687, Newton succeeded in joining these twin pillars of scientific thought. Newtonian mechanics, often described as the culmination of the Scientific Revolution, created a new philosophy of nature in which nature's machinery follows mathematical principles.

In the *Principia*, laid out in three books, Newton unified celestial and terrestrial motion under one set of mechanical principles that could be expressed mathematically; proposed new laws of motion, including his well-known third law, which states that for every action there is an equal and opposite reaction; proposed that all motion is linear; and theorized that the universe is infinite, not finite.

He resolved many difficult questions whose answers had eluded other mechanical philosophers; took mechanics into areas of science that had seemed out of its reach, including fluid dynamics; and was the first to describe the forces of universal gravitation. In this wide-ranging treatise, Newton established the theoretical framework for modern science and raised questions that would occupy scientists into the present.

The Impact of the Scientific Revolution on Science and Society

The distinction between science and society used in the title of this section is itself a product of the transition in thinking that took place during the period of history known as the Scientific Revolution. In many ways, philosophers and scientists had always been separate from the mainstream, because their interests took them into more esoteric areas of questioning and thinking. But they remained connected to the experience of everyday life, because it was the laboratory in which they worked. As long as the senses were appreciated as valuable tools of science, there was a link between daily life and the extraordinary world of ideas and concepts used to explain its mysteries.

That connection was broken by Descartes, who separated mind from matter. Cartesian dualism discounted sense experience and empirical evidence in favor of objective reality as defined by the rational analytic mind of the scientist. In other words, science claimed a superior role in describing "the ways things really are" as opposed to trusting "what we know from our own experience."

The advertising phrase "My doctor says, Mylanta.®" is a modern-day example of this belief in science's superior knowledge. Meanwhile, the current mind-body-spirit movement is reminding us of an important connection that was lost centuries ago.

This dualistic perspective is part of the legacy of the Scientific Revolution, as are the central role of mathematics in science and our preference for mechanistic thinking. In *Nature's Numbers*, Ian Stewart describes the important role of mathematics in science: "Mathematics is to nature as Sherlock Holmes is to evidence. . . . It is a more or less systematic way of digging out the rules and structures that lie behind some observed pattern or regularity, and then using those rules and structures to explain what's going on."[12]

The world of mathematics is a world of imagination and abstraction, where scientists explore the "what ifs" about nature, and many modern scientists are somewhat mellower about their belief in the absolute power of mathematics. But for those in the seventeenth century, who had just discovered its powers of explanation, mathematics supported their belief in objective deductive reasoning over intuition and experience. Through mathematics scientists reached logical conclusions about their observations.

Add to this the belief that the world is a huge machine, whose mechanisms must be understood and explained in mathematical terms, and you have the scientific worldview of the seventeenth century: *Nature is a huge machine that operates with order and precision, and whose understanding is accessible only to scientists through the power of mathematics.* In other words, reality is not how you perceive it. It is mechanistic, mathematical, and removed from everyday experience.

So, what was the impact of science's new view of itself and its knowledge on society? The immediate impact was probably minimal. Most of the people living in the seventeenth century were still relatively uneducated and not attuned to scientific thinking. But over time, as science, religion, and the state worked to balance their authority and power, they succeeded in creating and transmitting a worldview in which scientific discoveries were used to promote social order through the authority of the state and its ally, the Church.

Scientific certainties dulled society's sensitivity to nature's wild side and supported the Church's view that man's wild nature must be controlled. The interweaving of scientific and religious views created a world of cause-effect thinking, belief systems, and institutions that were fixed and inflexible.

It embedded in our European ancestors a belief that the world operates like a machine, with clockwork precision through a code of rules and consequences. It created a world of sameness—predictable, controlled, known—where acts of nature, plagues, social upheaval, and other forms of disorder were seen as aberrations in a world of order.

It created what I call the *snow dome effect:* a predictable world, occasionally shaken by the hand of fate, only to return to its meticulous order under a dome of certainty assured by science, religion, and the state. Only in the twentieth century have modern realities and new scientific discoveries jolted us from this mechanistic and unrealistic view of the change

In the next chapter we'll explore the reasons why we must give up our mechanistic constructs. And we'll see how the new science is freeing us from the straitjacket of linear thinking and giving us new ways to appreciate the relationship between order and the constantly changing world around us.

BUTTERFLIES AND HURRICANES

A truly stable system expects the unexpected, is prepared to be disrupted, waits to be transformed.

—TOM ROBBINS

Even Cowgirls Get the Blues

Wayne Gretzky, recognized as the world's best hockey player, says that the key to his success is that he doesn't skate toward the puck, but instead tries to anticipate where its going and get there ahead of it. The same thing could be said about great leaders—they anticipate where change is going and make sure their organizations get there first.

Here, at the transition point between millennia, we are faced with the challenge of anticipating and responding to change in a world that is increasingly more interconnected. As our need to anticipate change has become more urgent, science has made a quantum leap in its own understanding about the dynamics of change.

The new *science of chaos theory and complexity* is providing us with information about the dynamics of the real world in which our decisions are being made. And in addition to helping us anticipate and respond to change, the new science has provided us with another option—the ability to *influence* change as it is emerging.

With the new science we have an innovative model for developing *insight* about the present and *foresight* about the future. As we cross the threshold into the twenty-first century, we finally have a way to develop the much-needed skill of *strategic thinking*—a skill that will allow us to see and influence the future, today.

In order to lead change, you have to understand it. Just like athletes must understand their games. But until now, all we've had are techniques designed to stabilize what feels like an endless roller-coaster ride of change. This is like having a playbook without understanding the subtleties of the game that create the dynamic or constantly changing *field of play.*

In the last decade, a lot of effort has been focused on identifying and managing internal change processes designed to make organizations more competitive. This is known as *planned* change. You decide to do something different, such as *re*inventing, *re*structuring or *re*engineering, and develop a plan to carry it out. These are ongoing large-scale efforts designed to make organizations more effective in responding to the changes, challenges, and opportunities in their larger *external* environment.

Leaders, focused on organizational transformation, internal-change agents, and change-management consultants and trainers have worked together over the last ten years to build a library of case studies on successful internal change efforts. They have demonstrated what works and what doesn't. These experts in the *human side of change* have compiled playbooks filled with ideas, principles, processes, and techniques designed to help managers and employees build commitment to change and maintain productivity, while moving forward with the least amount of resistance.

But it's easy to let the *internal* change process become the primary focus of attention, because results are tangible and the process manageable, when compared to the constant changes and uncertainties swirling around outside the window. It feels safer to hunker down in familiar territory and wait out the storm. But we've all experienced that sudden unplanned something that seems to come out of nowhere, like a gust of wind that blows the door open. It forces us to drop what we're doing in order to come up with a quick and effective response. And we know from experience that when change comes as a surprise, it takes more resources to identify and implement an effective response. It also has the potential to create huge power outages or disconnections throughout an organization.

As the executive team changes its priorities or makes decisions that require the organization to move quickly, middle managers are still working on the last set of priorities in addition to the re-YouNameIt change process, while front-line employees are just beginning to get the message about changes needed two weeks ago. Everyone points to someone or something else as the source of confusion.

But is there another way to understand change? One that would get us out of this vicious fire-fighting cycle? One that stops the divisiveness and gets everyone on the same team? One that helps everyone understand the relationship between your internal change efforts and the complexities in the world around them? One that connects each person and each function to the organization's evolving A-list priorities? One that supports long-term strategies and quick maneuvers? One that helps us anticipate change, see the options, and make wise choices—before a crisis arises? And finally, one that allows us to create or influence change to our advantage?

The answer is YES. At last, we can take a deep breath and exhale.

If we lift our eyes and our thinking, everything we see and experience can be thought of as happening within a larger system. And the key to understanding the dynamics of the "big picture" is to see the larger system in a coherent and realistic way. Edward Lorenz, a research meteorologist and mathematician working at the Massachusetts Institute of Technology in the early 1960s, knew this as he started the next run on his computer and left the room to get a cup of coffee. Trying to come up with a weather model that would help meteorologists provide accurate forecasts was beginning to seem like a fool's game. All he had to do was look out the window to understand the futility of his efforts. While his weather models forecast the same weather day after day, the weather outside changed constantly. He was thinking about all of this as he sat back down at his desk.[1]

Lost in his own thoughts, it took him a minute or two to notice that something was different. Instead of the usual rolling pattern coming from the tracing device he had hooked up to his (what we would now call primitive) computer, the tracings were fluctuating wildly. The printout looked like the electrocardiogram (EKG) of a hospital patient whose heart is fibrillating out of control.

He tried to figure out what was going on. His intuition told him that something significant was happening, but as he replayed his actions just before leaving the room, nothing was different. He'd done everything just like he'd done it a hundred times before. Except, that he had abbreviated one of the numbers he was using to represent atmospheric conditions. Instead of .506127 he had rounded it to .506, typed it in, and left it to run while he walked down the hall to the coffeepot. What he discovered when he returned was one of the first clues to a new science that would revolutionize the way we think about change.

As we saw in the previous chapter, from the seventeenth century to the early part of this century science believed that the universe was static and operated like a huge machine with clockwork precision. Change, they believed, was caused by outside forces acting on solid lifeless particles of matter like the action of the cue ball on the eight ball in a game of pool. The universe, they believed, was characterized by order, which could be recognized, understood, and measured through the use of mathematics.

This classical mechanical-mathematical view of the world required that scientists develop narrowly focused research questions. Focusing their attention and then joining the results from one experiment to the results of the next was an approach based on the central tenet of the mechanistic view—only by understanding the parts could one make sense of the whole.

Mathematics is the basic language or tool that undergirds all scientific disciplines. It allows scientists to convert their questions from words to numbers and symbols. It's scientific shorthand, and it's a language we nonscientists have adapted for our own everyday uses. Without mathematics we would have a hard time balancing our checkbooks, giving directions, following a recipe, making a telephone call, or keeping track of who's winning the basketball game.

Math helps us make sense of and organize the world in very specific ways. One of the ways it does this is by helping us recognize patterns. For example, my editor's office in New York is easier to find by looking first for the coordinates "6th Avenue between 48th and 49th Streets," then for the street address, "1230 Avenue of the Americas (which is also 6th Ave.)," and finally for his location in that building, "11th floor." Each of these numbers helps me identify a pattern of organization that leads me to his door. Just like the number on your boarding pass tells you how to locate your seat on an airplane. Numbers are also clues that lead us to a point where we can see a pattern of organization. For example, every spring when we fill out the dreaded income tax forms, we are creating a picture of our financial pattern over the last year. In simple ways, numbers help us see and understand patterns, reach conclusions, and make decisions. This is also what they do for scientists.

Mathematics is the tool that helps scientists uncover the hidden patterns in nature, which are clues to how the world is organized and by what patterns of organization or principles it operates.[2] Mathematics is the imposition of man-made logic on nature's creation. It is a highly refined tool, but it is not reality.

Mathematical equations can at best only serve as highly idealized representations of events in the real world. As Benoit Mandelbrot, a pioneering mathematician working at IBM in the late 1960s and '70s, put it: "Clouds are not spheres, mountains are not cones, coastlines are not circles, and bark is not smooth, nor does lightning travel in a straight line."[3]

The techniques of mathematical *approximation*, the type of rounding and shaving implied by Mandelbrot's statement, were designed to help scientists screen out nature's irregularities and stabilize the variables in question in order to study them. This is similar to a carpenter's shaving and planing. A carpenter ignores the small differences and irregularities in a piece of lumber in favor its approximate linear qualities, which allow it to fit with the next board and the next, eventually forming the frame of a house. The underlying assumption is that small differences are insignificant, and in many cases that assumption proved to be *useful.* Translating the motions of planets, comets, or other natural phenomena into approximate linear equations provided scientists with new insights and led to many of science's great discoveries. But it also created the belief in a predictable, linear, cause-effect world in which overlooking small differences in favor of mathematical approximation was more than just useful, it defined reality.

In the early part of this century, the success of this approach led French scientist Marquis Pierre-Simon de Laplace and others to adopt a perspective known as scientific determinism, which says that through mathematics it is possible to predict everything that will happen by just knowing the existing conditions at an earlier point in time and projecting those into the future.[4] In a static mechanically efficient universe this perspective seemed to make sense.

Lorenz's weather program was based on this classical deterministic model. Given a set of approximate linear equations representing the weather conditions last Tuesday, it projected those into the future and came up with, guess what? A forecast that predicted approximately the same weather next Tuesday as last Tuesday, and every Tuesday after that into infinity. Clearly, something was missing.

What Lorenz discovered is that a deterministic system—a simple system which follows fixed, precise laws—can display what looks like erratic or random behavior because of its *sensitive dependence on initial conditions*. In the classic deterministic model, the future is merely an extension of the past. There is no room for chance, changing conditions, or creativity. It's a straight line from the present to the future. What Lorenz found is that in systems like the weather or the Indianapolis 500 a straight line is not the reality.

In *nonlinear dynamical* systems, the variables cannot be taken apart and added back together again like a child's building blocks; A+B does not equal C. In these types of systems, things never happen the same way twice. A small change in one variable will create changes in another and another, because the variables are interacting constantly and changing in response to each other. Lorenz discovered that nonlinear dynamical systems are teeming with creative potential and sensitivity to new influences. This sensitivity to new influences means that change can be introduced at almost any point. In other words, the possibilities for creativity, innovation, and change are infinite.

This *sensitive dependence on initial conditions*, he found, starts an interactive process known metaphorically as the *Butterfly Effect*. The Butterfly Effect describes the image of a butterfly flapping its wings in Asia and causing a hurricane in the Atlantic, which is a metaphor for how small changes or events create complex results. The Butterfly Effect was a major breakthrough in understanding how small systems interact with large systems. A small change in the initial conditions of one system multiply upward, expanding into larger and larger systems, changing conditions all along the way, eventually causing unexpected consequences at a broader level sometime in the future. That's why the slight difference in his weather model caused by rounding just one variable from .506127 to .506 was enough to create a thunderstorm instead of sun in next week's forecast. It also explains why the physical and psychological conditioning of athletes is so important. In a game of basketball, for example, the initial conditions are changing constantly as each player experiences varying levels of physical exhaustion, focus, and pressure to perform. In a sense, each player is a small system whose starting conditions at any point in time influence the dynamics of the next play and the next, eventually determining the outcome of the larger system—the overall game and its final score.

It would have been easy for Lorenz to stop here and give up any hope of developing a forecasting model for the weather. Nonlinearity had long been the nemesis of mathematicians, as nonlinear equations were almost impossible to solve. But setting aside his expertise as a meteorologist and listening to his instincts as a mathematician, he sensed something more. A sort of geometric architecture to the randomness in the weather tracings he'd produced by tinkering with the system's initial equations—an order within the disorder. So, he decided to follow his intuition by studying a simpler type of nonlinear system: convection.

Remember that Lorenz's original interest was in predicting the weather. So, in studying convection, the type of nonlinear heating, cooling, and rolling process that takes place when you add cream to a hot cup of coffee or when cool air touches a hot radiator, he was searching for a nonlinear system that could be represented by just a few equations. Since it was the future he was interested in, he wanted to see what would happen when he tried to predict the future state of a simple nonlinear system. He came up with a set of three equations that represented the variables in a simplified convection system and used his tracing device to create a *picture* of that system.

Lorenz used a technique that had been developed half a century before by French mathematician Jules-Henri Poincaré. Poincaré invented a mathematical concept known as phase space, where all the possible motions of a dynamical system could be represented by a geometric shape. By translating numbers into shapes he demonstrated that it is possible to create a picture of a system's behavior over time. Poincaré's geometrization of dynamics demonstrated the power of imagery in mathematics[5] and was an early predecessor to the recent field of scientific visualization—the ability to translate numbers into pictures through the use of high-speed computers and computer graphics.

This simple image, resembling the wings of a butterfly or an owl's mask, is known as the Lorenz Attractor. The most remarkable thing about this image is that it allowed scientists to *see*, for the first time, the order, shape, or structure hidden within the behavior of a nonlinear system. This is the picture that's worth a thousand words.

There are three important findings represented in this image. First, because the system is deterministic, it is possible to know its initial conditions. What's difficult, because the system is also nonlinear, is

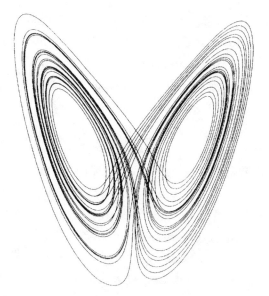

The Lorenz Attractor. The first picture of the order hidden within the behavior of a nonlinear system.

Compliments of Edward N. Lorenz.

predicting its future state. Because it is nonlinear, it would be easy to assume that its long term behavior would be random and disorderly. But remember that Lorenz's intuition told him that there was something hidden beneath the apparent randomness. So, using the three nonlinear equations for convection, he created a picture of the *behavior of the system over time.* This image represents all the possible outcomes of the three equations. And what it shows is that *there is a type of self-organizing pattern, shape, or structure that becomes obvious when the behavior of the system is seen as a whole. There is order hidden beneath the disorder.*

After you see the pattern, the obvious next question is "What creates the pattern and holds the system together?" *The pattern arises because the variables in the system are attracted to and interact with each other in a unique way.* The attraction of the variables creates the edges or boundaries of the pattern, and the interactive relationship of the variables creates the internal design that never repeats itself.

And finally, this image represents a shift made possible by the power of computer graphics. In the past, scientists and mathematicians would try to *solve* nonlinear equations or *predict* the future of a nonlinear system in terms of a singular outcome or state. What this image shows us is that *while it may not be possible to solve or predict the future of a nonlinear system, it is possible to provide a qualitative description of its characteristics and behavior as a whole over time.* Ian Stewart describes this shift in perspective: "[T]his approach again changes the meaning of 'solve.' First that word meant 'find a formula.' Then its meaning changed to 'find approximate numbers.' Finally, it has in effect become 'tell me what the solutions look like.' . . .[T]his move toward an explicitly qualitative theory is not a retreat but a major advance. For the first time, we are starting to understand nature's patterns in their own terms."[6] Analyzing a nonlinear system by describing its behavior and characteristics as a whole over time is known as qualitative analysis.

Although Lorenz is now recognized as one of the earliest pioneers in the development of *chaos theory,* a new type of mathematics explaining the complex behavior of nonlinear systems, the implications of his work were not immediately understood. In a sense they were isolated findings in a field still being fertilized for the harvest to come.

Until recently, the different scientific disciplines and specialties did not communicate between and among themselves. It's as if each were a smokestack operating independently from the others. Their research intermingled only when someone stood outside and looked for similarities across the columns of smoke drifting into the atmosphere. And what one would have seen, beginning in the early part of this century, were the sparks of a revolution in the making.

The strict deterministic view of the world promoted by Laplace began to shift in the early part of the twentieth century. Einstein's theory of general relativity, which he proposed in 1915, provided a new theory of gravity based on the idea that space-time is not flat, but curved. In his theory, both space and time are not static, but *dynamic,* affecting and affected by everything that happens in the universe.[7] This was a dramatic departure from the fixed deterministic view of the universe supported by Laplace, and it paved the way for Edwin Hubble's discovery in 1929 that the universe is not static, but expanding in all directions.

This discovery opened the door for rapid advances in astronomy and physics. Max Planck's quantum theory of energy and Werner Heisenberg's uncertainty principle led to a reformulation of mechanics known as quantum mechanics or quantum physics, which describes the behavior of particles at the subatomic level. Stated simply, quantum physics says that the smallest particles are not solid static lifeless bits of matter, but are instead pulsating bundles of energy known as quanta, whose behavior is impossible to measure or predict with absolute certainty, because they exist and interact in a quantum or energetic state that has a number of potential outcomes.[8]

In quantum physics, you can observe an outcome but only make guesses about the interactions of the particles involved and the path they took to that result. Quantum physics is based on a type of mathematics that helps scientists identify *probabilities*. The probabilities or potential outcomes arise out of the *dynamics* of the whole.

The recognition that the fundamental structure of the universe is dynamic behavior expressed as a whole, through its interconnections and relationships, was a dramatic departure from classical mechanics, where the parts determine the actions of the whole. With quantum physics, Laplace's fixed deterministic universe was replaced by an active universe filled with energy, interconnections, and creative potential. The linear, clockwork view of the world was transformed by science's recognition that at its most fundamental level the world is an energetic field of connections, relationships, and patterns of interaction. This discovery raised a whole set of new questions. If, at its most basic level, the world is made out of particles whose structure is actually expressed as a web of energetic relationships and patterns of interaction, what are the implications for how we view life at the macro level?

As much as science tries to be exact, it never can be. Science is an ongoing spiral of discovery, contradictions, gaps, partial answers, conclusions, and more discovery. Exploring nature is like trying to put together a jigsaw puzzle without the picture on the box top to guide you. The important thing to recognize is that gaps and inconsistencies generate new questions, which lead to new discoveries. For example, quantum physics and Einstein's theory of gravity, known as general relativity, are recognized as two of the three major scientific revolutions this century (chaos theory is the third), but they are inconsistent with each other. The search for a grand unified theory (GUT), which scientists believe will reconcile them, is one of science's greatest challenges.

Examples of other discoveries and theories that helped to lay the foundation for a whole new way of thinking about change include the discovery that our galaxy is only one among an infinite number of galaxies still being discovered today by the increasing power of land-based and satellite-based telescopes; the discovery of dense gravitational fields known as black holes; the discovery of dark matter, that unknown something that makes up an estimated 90 percent of the universe; the discovery of other planets with evidence of life-supporting elements; and the theory of an explosion, known as the Big Bang, which brought the universe into being.

While the disciplines of astronomy and physics moved forward, important advances were also being made in other scientific disciplines. For example, the biological theory of evolution, developed by Charles Darwin and first published in 1859, provided an explanation about how change occurs within and across species. Over the years, this theory has grown from its original concepts of random mutation and natural selection, also known as the survival of the fittest, to include the current ideas of niche adaptation and punctuated equilibrium.[9]

Modern evolutionary biologists believe that plants and animals adapt to their specific location, function, and set of circumstances within a complex living ecosystem, which itself survives and adapts as a whole through its intricate network of interdependent relationships. Today the exciting scientific debates are not over the validity of the theory, as they were in its earlier days, although the creationists occasionally stir that pot, but over the *dynamics* or "hows," of the process.

For well over a century, evolution has been the biological model for the development of life on earth and, with acceptance of the Big Bang theory in the early 1970s, it became the model for the development of the universe as a whole. Evolutionary biology and evolutionary cosmology converged to create a new model within which to explore nature's creativity—one more step in the breakthrough that was to come.

The natural world is filled with a variety of rich textures, shapes, and patterns—the rough bark on a tree, the long graceful limbs of a fern, stepping-stones across a stream. Yet, the richness of the real world could only be appreciated in the abstract by classical science. Scientists could identify the elements in a molecule of water, H_2O, but not the dynamics at work in a waterfall. New approaches were needed for exploring mysteries that they saw all around them—variations in cloud patterns, fluctuations in weather and wildlife populations, and changes in the rate and flow of mountain streams.

The common wisdom among scientists, even into the late 1970s, was that these questions could not be answered. Questions such as these were nonlinear and involved looking at the irregularities that mathematical approximation tried to screen out, as well as at a number of interdependent connections and relationships that scientists traditionally tried to break into component parts. In other words, these types of questions were better left unasked, because they were too frustrating. Science did not have the tools or the type of mathematics that would make these questions solvable.

By the early 1970s, science had become highly specialized and compartmentalized. Each discipline had many subspecialties pursuing very narrow lines of research with little communication among them. The narrower the research, the greater the prestige. Answering broad everyday questions required dealing directly with nature's unruliness. So instead, scientists developed their infamous "ivory tower" image by isolating themselves from the day-to-day by pursuing highly specialized research questions, which conformed more easily to mathematical modeling. Fueling this approach was the stiff competition for research funds, the lifeblood of any scientist, which were also focused at this more esoteric level.

But even with intense pressure to conform, there were renegades, scientists who were growing bored and restless with safe and what they considered irrelevant science. What they longed for was a new form of scientific freedom. Observing the world through a microscope with higher and higher levels of magnification is one way to learn. But these restless ones recognized that this approach eliminated much of the world outside their windows. They began to ask themselves if another approach could work. Could you also learn by stepping back and observing the world through a wide-angle lens? What could be learned by tackling those nightmarish nonlinear questions about nature's irregularities?

Those who would later be recognized as *chaos* pioneers began to probe these questions, even though they were warned against this by their colleagues. Like explorers facing unknown territory, they each followed their inner urgings and moved forward. Physics, biology, mathematics, astronomy, meteorology—all provided paths, first into *chaos* and then into *complexity*.

In everyday language the word "chaos" is used to describe conditions that appear to be highly disorganized, turbulent, or volatile. It's an active word that implies changeability and movement. It's a word used more and more to describe the state of world affairs. Now science has given it a new and deeper meaning.

Chaos theory is the popular name for dynamical systems theory, or nonlinear studies. Nonlinear dynamical systems are systems that, like the weather, move, grow, or change. It's difficult to predict the outcome or future state of a nonlinear system, because the variables are interacting and changing constantly in response to each other. The behavior of a nonlinear system is not a straight line. As it turns out, *most of the world is made up of nonlinear systems* and dynamical systems theory, or chaos theory is a new mathematical approach that allows scientists to study the *behavior* of nonlinear systems.

The weather along the eastern slope of the Rocky Mountains is a good example of a nonlinearity. Meteorologists there struggle to provide the public with at least a hint of what to expect during the day. Cold air, flowing down into the United States from Canada, collides near Denver with the warm jet stream air, creating volatile moisture and temperature conditions so extreme that in the foothills it's not unusual to see a cloudless blue sky turn gray with a sudden snow shower and then blue again, all within half an hour.

Over the last three decades, many individuals contributed to the development of chaos theory. Through their research, and the use of high-speed computers and computer graphics, scientists began to see and understand the dynamics at work behind the apparent randomness of nonlinear systems, and the pieces of the puzzle began to fit together. New concepts, techniques, and descriptions of nonlinear systems started to appear in research papers worldwide, eventually forming the framework for this new approach to answering those frustrating questions about nonlinearity. And this is what they found.

Most of the world is made up of nonlinear dynamical systems. The world is more nonlinear than it is linear, and nonlinear dynamical systems have several unique properties that make them recognizable. *First, beneath the seemingly chaotic behavior of a nonlinear system, there is order.* The term "order" does not refer to characteristics such as quiet, calm, or good, but refers instead to a type of self-organizing pattern, shape, or structure. The shape is created by the attraction or active relationship of the variables making up the system.

The concepts of attractor and attraction are important to understand. In its purest definition, an *attractor* is the end state or final behavior toward which a dynamical system moves. And that end state is either predictable or unpredictable. A *predictable attractor* is the end state into which a system *settles.* For example, if you throw a handful of marbles into a bowl, they will eventually all come to rest at the bottom. The bottom of the bowl is the attractor, a specific point. In other cases, the attractor is a cycle, as in the back-and-forth movement of a pendulum in a grandfather clock. You cannot predict the path of each marble nor the immediate behavior of a pendulum brought to a standstill by a mischievous child who grabs the swinging arm and then gives it a hard push. But you can predict the final outcome or behavior of each system: a pool of marbles at the bottom of the bowl and the pendulum's eventual return to cyclic motion.

Then there are *chaotic systems that never settle into a predictable or steady state* and those are said to have *strange attractors.* A graphic representation of such a system will reveal a complicated pattern or shape, where the internal design never repeats itself. Chaos theory describes the behavior of chaotic nonlinear systems and their strange attractors.

The Lorenz Attractor is a strange attractor, as would be the attractor for a hurricane. A tornado is another example of an energy system held together by a strange attractor. No external container or funnel gives a tornado its unique form. This dynamic, coherent, and focused system with a recognizable shape is created by the interaction of the variables making up the tornado. The attraction and force of the variables hold the system together and move it along its path of destruction at speeds of up to 200 miles per hour or more until it eventually loses its energy and disperses.

You may sense some flexibility in how the term strange attractor is used. The term "strange attractor" describes the behavior of the force or forces that hold the system variables in place. The strange attractor coalesces the energy and creates the system boundaries, while at the same time allowing dynamic activity within those boundaries. The shape of a hurricane or tornado provides evidence that a strange attractor is present, as do computer-generated pictures such as the Lorenz Attractor, which demonstrates the behavior of a chaotic system over time. The pictures provide evidence that a strange attractor exists. And because each strange attractor creates a unique shape, it is common to also hear the picture referred to as a "strange attractor."

Imagine walking down Main Street in the town where you live. You see a seemingly mismatched couple strolling arm in arm. What is the attraction that keeps them together? People usually are attracted to each other for many reasons. Those reasons or elements create an attraction that holds their relationship together. And like the dynamics in a game of basketball, all of those elements are interacting constantly to create the dynamics of the overall system or relationship. If we could create a graphic image of their relationship over time, it would have its own unique shape, or strange attractor.

If we translated these concepts into the business world, we would ask ourselves "What elements create the dynamics of a business or an industry and give it its unique shape and characteristics? What connections and relationships hold the system together and create the structure beneath the visible activity?" Understanding that beneath disorder there is order allowed scientists to look at the world with new eyes and ask new questions. How does the order or structure arise?

Lorenz discovered that nonlinear systems display *a sensitive dependence on initial conditions. Nonlinear systems, he found, are teeming with creative potential and sensitivity to new influences.* Because of this sensitivity to new influences, change can be introduced at almost any point, and the possibilities for creativity and innovation are infinite. He also found that through the Butterfly Effect, small changes multiply upward, expanding into larger and larger systems, changing conditions all along the way, eventually causing unexpected consequences at a broader level sometime in the future. *A nonlinear system responds to changes in itself through a type of feedback loop, set in motion by the Butterfly Effect. Through this process, small changes can produce complex results.*

An example of the Butterfly Effect occurs in the movie *Outbreak*, when an African monkey is brought to the United States and sold illegally to an exotic animal trader. Unknown to everyone, the monkey is carrying the deadly Ebola virus. The drama begins when the monkey infects its owner through a scratch on the arm, setting in motion a viral outbreak that threatens to kill the entire U.S. population within days. The scratch on the arm was a small event that multiplied up and out with enormous consequences.

As scientists began to understand the dynamics of nonlinear systems, they began to ask more questions about the interactions in and among systems. How do changes, such as evolution, fluctuations, and extinction, occur? What other dynamics are involved? *How do order and structure arise in the midst of constant change?* These questions brought them to the next level of understanding and to the concept of *complex adaptive systems.*

Complex adaptive systems (CAS) are open nonlinear evolutionary systems, such as a rain forest, that are constantly processing and incorporating new information. Their existence and structure depend on the constant flow of energy and new information, making it *impossible to know all of the initial conditions at any point in time.* These are systems that exist at the boundary between chaos and order. Instead of settling into a predictable or steady state like the back and forth motion of a pendulum, or ultimately dissipating like a hurricane or tornado, these types of systems adapt to change, thus their name *complex* adaptive *systems.*

In a complex adaptive system, change is constant because of the flow of new information, but dramatic change occurs when something tips the balance. *If* the system is sensitive to the new information, it goes through a period of *adaptation* out of which a new pattern or shape *emerges.* And, sometimes the changes are dramatic enough to be recognized as transformative—the system before the change is vastly different from the system after the change.

Imagine looking at a National Geographic video about a South American rainforest. It is humid, lush with vegetation and filled with the sounds of birds and other animals. It remains in this state of dynamic or active equilibrium until new information enters the system. Something happens to disturb it, such as commercial plant harvesting. Now, in your mind fast-forward the tape. You see that because the rain forest was sensitive to the new information, it has been pushed into a chaotic period or a period of instability.

Fast-forward the scene again to a place ten years in the future. Here you see that *adaptation* has occurred and a new state of equilibrium has been reached. Some plants and animals are gone, but others are thriving and new species or hybrids have emerged. The rain forest has adapted to the *edge of chaos,* poised and ready for new information.

Evolutionary biology is providing new insights about how systems such as this evolve and adapt. Stuart Kauffman reminds us that "the edge-of-chaos image arises in coevolution as well, for as we evolve, so do our competitors; to remain fit, we must adapt to their adaptations."[10]

Chaos theory describes how a sensitive dependence on initial conditions contains the potential for change through the Butterfly Effect. Complexity theory describes how order and structure arise through the process of adaptation set in motion by new information, which tips the balance and pushes the system into a chaotic episode. In complex adaptive systems, complexity theory incorporates and depends on the details of chaos theory. In other words, chaos is not something that just happens in an otherwise orderly world. It is the mechanism through which change is initiated and organized. It is the way the world creates the rich diversity that we see all around us.

In summary:

- We do not live in a static, linear cause-effect world. We live in a world made up of nonlinear dynamical systems. Our world is full of motion, change, and emerging events.

- The world may appear to be disorderly. But beneath the apparent disorder there is order. The term "order" does not refer to characteristics such as quiet, calm, or good, but refers instead to a self-organizing pattern, shape, or structure.

- The patterns or shapes are created by the attraction or active relationship of the elements or components of the system.

- We may experience disorder, but we need to ask ourselves, What is beneath the surface? What connections, relationships, and patterns of interaction are creating the structure beneath the visible activity?

- Because nonlinear systems display a *sensitive dependence on initial conditions,* a small event in one system can cause tremendous turbulence in another through the Butterfly Effect.

- In *complex adaptive systems,* which have the ability to process and incorporate new information, change occurs through a process of *adaptation.* Through this process a new self-organizing pattern or shape emerges.

3

GETTING STARTED:
REAL WORLD APPLICATIONS

What everyone knows is what has already happened or become

obvious. What the aware individual knows is what has not yet

taken shape, what has not yet occurred. Everyone says victory

in battle is good, but if you see the subtle and notice the hidden

so as to seize victory where there is no form, that is really good.

—SUN TZU

The Art of War

Starting in the summer of 1989, the desire for freedom by oppressed peoples held us spellbound in front of our television sets. From Tiananmen Square to Berlin, the struggle for democracy captured our hearts and our imaginations. Who can forget the gripping image of one brave man standing alone in front of an armored tank in Tiananmen Square or pictures of the Berlin Wall being taken apart piece by piece? Through these events, we and the geopolitical world were transformed.

While the student demonstrations in China ended in bloodshed, the revolution that swept through Eastern Europe was relatively peaceful. And the symbolic dismantling of the Berlin Wall in November 1989 marked the end of the Cold War between the Soviet Union and the United States and its allies in Western Europe. How did this happen?

What circumstances created this revolution and allowed it to move with lightning-bolt speed?

The fall of communism in the former Soviet Union and throughout Eastern Europe was set in motion long before its final collapse by factors such as the arms race forced by President Reagan; Mikhail Gorbachev's election and his policies of *glasnost* (openness) and *perestroika* (restructuring); and the Chornobyl nuclear disaster. But the underlying initial condition that finally erupted and changed the course of history was the strength of the Polish worker's union—Solidarity.

Through its efforts, Solidarity initiated the first transfer of power to a noncommunist government in a Soviet bloc country. This show of strength, more than any other factor, coalesced the deep-seated desire for freedom that finally toppled the Wall. It was an historic regional event with enormous political and economic repercussions worldwide.

Throughout history the world has been transformed by the availability and use of information. From the invention of the wheel to each new iteration of the microprocessor, innovation, information, and change have transformed the world from simple farming communities into complex industrial and technological societies.

The Apollo space missions of the late 1960s gave us the first pictures of the Earth as a globe and the first look at our planet from the surface of the moon. A new worldview began to take shape as we and millions of other people around the world studied those images of Earth reflected back to us as a seamless whole.

Thinking of ourselves as separated by political, economic, and cultural boundaries began to shift toward thinking of ourselves as connected across boundaries. A global vocabulary began to emerge and now, as we look toward the twenty-first century, global thinking is part of mainstream strategic thinking.

The ability to receive, process, and incorporate new information has created a global environment that is in effect one vast system with many interconnecting points. Through television we have seen live rescue operations following the earthquakes in Los Angeles and San Francisco and floods in the Midwest and the South. During the Persian Gulf War we heard the sounds of people huddled in bomb shelters as missiles exploded in the background. And we shared the hopes and prayers of a peace treaty signed after years of fighting in the Middle East.

Lorenz demonstrated through his weather models that a small event in one sector can cause tremendous turbulence in another. In the same way, a small change in social, economic, or technological conditions can have a tremendous impact on a business. Because of this sensitivity to new influences, the biggest challenge facing any type of organization today is finding a way to keep up with the rate of change—to process and incorporate new information before a crisis arises.

For example, the banking industry, like the rain forest, has had to adapt to changes in its environment—new technology, including on-line banking, changes in customer needs and expectations, regulation, the economy and new forms of competition. Everyday it seems poised *at the edge of chaos,* and in the last few years it has been pushed over the edge into periods of instability and rapid adaptation by a series of bank megamergers.

On-line services also have affected travel agents, mortgage brokers, real estate agents, stockbrokers, and insurance sales agents. These industries are sensitive to changes in electronic information services, but not necessarily to changes in the food industry like the development of fat substitutes such as Olestra.

If we could create a detailed graphic image of the global environment, it would be filled with systems, each represented by a unique pattern or strange attractor. If we could visualize the interactions of industries, systems, issues, and new developments, we would see strange attractors colliding with others to create change, adaptation, and new patterns of interaction. Organizations, industries, and societies are influenced and restructured through these Butterfly-like interactions. I often imagine this to look like the changing colors and patterns used in various screen-saver software.

In addition to strange attractors that are already fully formed, new ones may also arise out of your system's emerging initial conditions. Strange attractors may take the form of events, interactions, or developments that coalesce energy and focus attention. They introduce new stimuli into a system, which start a multiplying process much like that of the Butterfly Effect. The proposed 1993 merger of Bell Atlantic and TCI was a strange attractor that pointed the telecommunications industry in a new direction. "You can't underestimate the impact of this one on future deals. It created the climate we're all working in," said Charles Dolan, founder of Cablevision Systems Corporation, in an early 1994 *Wall Street Journal* article.[1]

For TCI and Bell Atlantic, the decision to attempt a merger was based on their ability to see new technology "perking," or just beginning to take shape, and the impending convergence of many electronic technologies on the horizon. *"Perking" information is the term I use to identify the new initial conditions to which your system may be sensitive—changes or developments that are already taking shape just below the surface, and which can only be seen with peripheral vision or well-developed foresight skills.* These are things which may seem small now, but if any one of them mushroomed overnight it could have a dramatic impact on the future of your business.

The key to foresight is learning to recognize your system's initial conditions as they are emerging, so that you can see change coming, respond early, or influence it to your advantage. *It's important to recognize your system's initial conditions BEFORE they erupt as an unexpected strange attractor.*

With their proposed merger, Bell Atlantic and TCI were attempting to influence the future by creating an organization with the technical and financial resources to take advantage of emerging technology and what they defined as the business of the future—"the electronic transfer of information into homes." By being first to identify, define, and act on the reconfiguration of the telecommunications industry, they changed the environment of an industry overnight.

An event that acts as a strange attractor will quickly give visibility to unrecognized initial conditions—concerns or developments perking within a society or an industry. The Clarence Thomas–Anita Hill hearings before the judiciary committee of the United States Senate are a good example of a strange attractor that tapped into an unrecognized field of concern regarding sexual harassment.

Following those hearings at the end of 1991, the political landscape changed dramatically. A record number of women were elected to public office in 1992, numerous charges of sexual harassment were filed against public officials and corporate executives, and businesses quickly began reviewing their policies related to sexual harassment in the workplace.

In a similar way, the O. J. Simpson trial coalesced issues related to domestic violence and the impact of money and the media on our judicial process. As a result of this case, social service and legal experts all across the country are proposing faster hearings, more serious penalties for first-time offenders, and greater protection for women and children who are victims of domestic violence.

Strange attractors can force paradigm shifts. With the introduction of user-friendly personal computers into the business market, Apple Computer created a paradigm shift to which others in the industry had to respond. By providing personalized desktop computing power, Apple quickly shifted the paradigm away from large central and technically complicated mainframe computers. It was a small company that created tremendous turbulence in IBM's backyard.

This is an example of what Andrew Grove in his book *Only the Paranoid Survive* calls a "strategic inflection point." According to Grove, a strategic inflection point is a point of bifurcation, where a fundamental or very large change occurs in your business environment, shifting it in a new direction.[2] A change of this magnitude would have the same impact on a business or an industry as a 7.5 earthquake or a 60-foot tidal wave would have on a busy port city like Seattle. In other words, the post–inflection point landscape is dramatically different from the one that existed before the inflection point.

In his book, Grove describes the impact of containerization on the shipping industry:

> In the span of a decade, a virtual instant in the history of shipping, the standardization of shipbuilding designs, the creation of refrigerated transport ships and, most importantly, the evolution of containerization—a technology which permitted easy transfer of cargo on and off ships—introduced a "10X" change in the productivity of shipping, reversing an inexorably rising trend in costs. . . . [S]ome ports made the change, others tried but couldn't, and many resolutely fought this trend. Consequently, the new technologies led to a worldwide reordering of shipping ports. . . . Ports that didn't adopt the new technologies [as Singapore and Seattle did] have become candidates for redevelopment into shopping malls, recreation areas and waterfront apartment complexes.[3]

A strange attractor is an issue, event, or new development to which your system is sensitive, like the shipping industry was sensitive to containerization. Remember, strange attractors may arise out of your system's perking information or *emerging initial conditions*—changes or developments that are already taking shape just below the surface. And there are three important reasons to pay attention to this type of information.

First, these underlying or perking conditions may erupt into a powerful strange attractor and catch you off guard, giving you little or no time to influence what is emerging. When this happens all you can do is respond, and the cost in terms of time and dollars is usually much higher. Nothing underscores this more clearly than the answer given by Lou Gerstner, IBM's chairman and CEO, in response to questions about the company's record $23 billion-dollar loss over a two-year (1992–93) period: "If there is one thing that best summarizes what happened to IBM, it's that we missed changes in the marketplace.... We failed to adapt quickly to fundamental change in the marketplace."[4] At the time of this statement, IBM was paying the price for its failure to respond soon enough to Apple Computer and its intention to shift the market toward user-friendly desktop computing.

Second, perking information may help you identify a product or service gap or an unrecognized field of opportunity for something new. In the automobile industry, the success of the sports utility vehicle is an example of a product category that tapped into a perking field of desire for more leisure time and adventure in the lives of tired midlife baby boomers. By tapping into the changing *initial conditions* of an entire generation, companies have an opportunity to create the strange attractor—the new product or service, which becomes a "must have" for millions.

But most important, recognizing your system's initial conditions as they are emerging gives you an opportunity to influence what is beginning to take shape, as was the case with Bell Atlantic and TCI. In other words, *if you want to influence the future, you need to identify your system's perking information or changing initial conditions—and apply your resources there. These are your new leverage points.*

A story taken from World War II illustrates the importance of paying attention to what's perking just below the surface. After traveling through Europe on a family vacation in 1936, Paul Galvin, founder of Galvin Manufacturing Company, known since 1947 as Motorola, was convinced that a major European war was just over the horizon. He was correct. And in 1940, a year after the war started and the year before the Japanese attack on Pearl Harbor pushed the United States into World War II, Galvin asked one of his engineers to find out what kind of battle-field communications devices were being used by the U.S. Army.[5]

What he found was that the army relied on awkward, wire-dependent transmission devices. So without a contract and before the United States actually entered the war, Galvin Manufacturing responded to the perking need for a wireless communications device. By the time the United States entered the war in late 1941, the first model, a short-range, portable, handheld radio known as the Handie-Talkie, was already in production and in high demand.

Feedback from the troops in Europe led to other models of "walkie-talkies," with ranges of ten or more miles. Galvin's communications products gave the United States a strategic advantage in military operations abroad and made it possible to create the first civil defense communications networks at home. Galvin's innovative, anticipatory approach to a perking need increased company sales from $10 million to $80 million in just four years, tripled its workforce, and established the company as an industry leader with a reputation for foresight, innovation, quality, and performance.

Through these examples, we see that successful strategic thinking has two major components: *insight* about the present and *foresight* about the future. And the key to both is understanding the *dynamics* of the "big picture" context in which your decisions are being made.

The new science of chaos theory and complexity is helping us understand the business environment in a coherent and realistic way. Of the many new concepts and techniques that helped scientists understand the dynamics of change in complex adaptive systems, there are seven that when used together provide the framework for strategic thinking as defined by the new science.

THE SEVEN PRINCIPLES OF STRATEGIC THINKING AS DEFINED BY THE NEW SCIENCE

1. Look at whole systems, not just their parts.
2. There is a relationship between order and disorder, and self-organizing change occurs as a result of their interactions.
3. A small event in one sector can cause tremendous turbulence in another.

4. Maps, models, and visual images make it easier to see connections, relationships, and patterns of interaction.

5. Scanning across disciplines and industries is the key to seeing emerging conditions, paradigm shifts, and opportunities for innovation.

6. Nonlinear thinking is critical to recognizing clues about changes in the environment.

7. Perspective is important when viewing chaotic events.

In Part II of this book we'll explore a new model for strategic thinking and planning based on the dynamics of change as described by the new science, the seven principles, the process of *visual thinking*, and the use of a new tool—a *FutureScape*™.

PART TWO

THE ART AND SCIENCE OF
VISUAL THINKING

VISUAL THINKING

*Our imagination is stretched to the utmost, not as in fiction, to imagine things that are not really there, but just to comprehend those things which **are** there.*

—RICHARD FEYNMAN

The Character of Physical Law

When I was in high school, a boy in the class ahead of me, Ken Healey (now M.D.), conducted an experiment that demonstrated the power of *thinking in pictures* and won a national award for achievement in scientific research. Through a series of photographs, he showed the effects of the drug LSD on the ability of spiders to weave their webs.

The beautiful geometric patterns we are used to seeing became tangled distorted messes after he administered the drug. Everyone who saw those pictures understood immediately the dangers of LSD, years before its actual chemical effects on the brain were identified. Pictures were a bridge to understanding.

In a similar way, the Lorenz Attractor is the picture that represents a thousand words. This simple image allowed scientists to see and understand what had been impossible to comprehend through mathematical modeling alone.

It was scientific intuition that pulled Lorenz and other chaos pioneers in a new direction. But it was computer graphics that allowed them to see the order hidden within disorder.

Thinking in pictures helps us link our intuitive sense of events in the world with our intellectual understanding. Now, more than ever, we need to integrate the techniques of imagination and the skill of intuition with our analytic competencies to help us see and understand the complexities that perplex and vex us daily. Visualization *is the key to in*sight *and fore*sight—*and the next revolution in strategic thinking and planning.*

Pictures and images have the power to convey both content and meaning. Who can forget the stricken face of Oklahoma City fireman Chris Fields as he held Baylee Almon in her last minutes of life? Or the look of satisfaction and pain on the face of U.S. Olympic gymnast Kerri Strug, as she vaulted her team to gold while sacrificing her chance for an individual medal? Or pictures from Chicago's Brookfield Zoo showing Binti, a female gorilla, gently cradling a toddler who had just fallen 18 feet into her cage?

We are a visual society, yet there are some things we just don't see. For example, recently NBC News reported a story called, "What America's Schools Didn't See Coming." The story was based on information released by the U.S. Department of Education announcing that grades K through 12 will set enrollment records each year until 2006.

From 1996–2006, there will be an estimated 55 million new enrollments requiring 190,000 more teachers, 6,000 new schools, and expenditures of $15 billion each year. Four factors were blamed for this situation:

1. Baby Boom Echo: children of baby boomers (1946–64), who married and parented late;
2. Increased pregnancy rates among minorities;

3. Immigration, primarily Hispanic and Asian;
4. Declining high school dropout rates nationwide.

The president and the U.S. Department of Education immediately called this a national crisis requiring urgent attention.

Now, my question is "Why didn't someone see this coming?" Statistics are kept in each of these four areas. So, you'd think that teachers, administrators, community leaders, and especially the state and federal departments responsible for education would have seen the trends, recognized a potential convergence, and developed a response plan, before the situation reached crisis proportions.

We might be tempted to call this incompetence, except that "surprise" events and circumstances are widespread. Everyday the *Wall Street Journal* and other business and trade publications carry stories about executives struggling with unexpected crises that with hindsight seem foreseeable.

Again, what prevents us from seeing what seems so obvious? I'm sure there are many answers, but I believe the primary reason is that we don't know how to see or visualize the multiple complexities—relationships, connections, patterns of interaction, and subtle changes—that are creating the *dynamics* of the real world in which our decisions are being made.

We rely instead on quantitative data and analysis to provide us with information about a constantly changing environment. We rely on snapshots to create the motion picture. We depend on the parts to tell us about the whole. And we rely on information tracking, which helps us see the trees but not the forest.

Scientists faced a similar dilemma, until computer graphics allowed them to see the behavior of nonlinear systems. When computers reached the point where numbers could be converted into pictures, they were able to think about and explore the world in new ways. For scientists, visualization, through the integration of high-speed computation and colorful 3-D graphics, has become the new indispensable tool of insight.

Likewise in business, sophisticated computer graphics are being used to study quantitative data. But so far, computers lack the technology to look out the window, scan the horizon, and create an accurate representation of the business environment.

The truth is that only the human mind is capable of dealing with the level of complexity in today's world. But how do we develop our ability to work effectively in this new arena?

In his classic text on strategic thinking, *The Mind of the Strategist*, Kenichi Ohmae writes, "Great strategies, like great works of art or great scientific discoveries, call for technical mastery in the working out but originate in insights that are beyond the realm of conscious analysis."[1] So, let's take a look at the ways in which great minds work.

■ ■ ■

Decades before space travel became a reality, Albert Einstein imagined himself as a "man in a box" traveling through the universe on a ray of light. This imaginary journey helped him develop the theory of general relativity and ensured that his name would forever be associated with the word "genius."

■ ■ ■

Since 1963, amyotrophic lateral sclerosis (ALS) has claimed his ability to walk, write, and speak without assistance, but Stephen Hawking's mind is very much intact. While his body grew weaker, he used his mind to challenge and expand our view of the universe by imagining a Big Bang, the dynamics of a newly formed universe, and the behavior of black holes. And now as he works on a grand unified theory to reconcile relativity and quantum physics, he is easily recognized as the most brilliant theoretical physicist of our time.

■ ■ ■

His father taught him that to name a bird is not the same as knowing the bird. This childhood lesson influenced every aspect of Richard Feynman's life. Whether studying physics, drumming, sketching, traveling to remote parts of the world, investigating the Challenger disaster, or preparing for his own death from cancer, every undertaking was an exuberant quest to "know the thing."

His ability to visualize and diagram the basic principles of quantum electrodynamics revolutionized physics. The Feynman Diagrams, as they became known, helped physicists and students of physics understand the dynamics at work beneath the complex mathematical equations they used to name things.

■ ■ ■

Internationally recognized animal welfare advocate and Colorado State University professor Temple Grandin designs and evaluates livestock-handling facilities in her head without even a preliminary pencil sketch. She explains, "Every design problem I've ever solved started with my ability to visualize and see the world in pictures. . . . I don't need a fancy graphics program that can produce three-dimensional design simulations. I can do it better and faster in my head."[2]

■ ■ ■

In these four examples, the common thread to insight was *visual thinking: the ability to create and interact with images in one's mind.* It is a highly developed natural talent found in many who are recognized for their original works. But until now, it has not been well understood even by those whose work defines it.

How we think is not something we usually think about. But in recent years, most of us have learned something about different thinking styles through the popularized version of Roger Sperry's 1981 Nobel Prize–winning research, which was started in the 1960s. While working with individuals whose epilepsy had been surgically treated by disconnecting the major communication channels between the brain's two hemispheres, Sperry, a neuropsychologist working at the California Institute of Technology, demonstrated that each hemisphere is responsible for a unique constellation of functions.[3]

The right hemisphere recognizes color, music, images, symbols, patterns, and three-dimensional spatial relationships. It understands the gestalt, context, or impression of the whole as well as concepts, meaning, and emotion. The left hemisphere specializes in language, logic, and the use of quantitative tools. It helps us perform sequential tasks and focus on content and details.

In a healthy brain working as a whole, the brain's specialized functions are relatively indistinct. In Sperry's unique split-brain population, the hidden differences revealed themselves and could be more clearly delineated. The findings, therefore, had important clinical and cognitive implications.

For neurologists, the findings assisted in the diagnosis and treatment of functional deficits caused by disease, stroke, or other types of brain injury. For psychologists, the findings confirmed and expanded earlier research demonstrating a biological basis for mental processes.

These exciting new results provided a foundation for all types of spin-off research, adding to the pool of information about hemispheric differentiation. But many pointed to the research findings as proof of the age-old belief in a fundamental dichotomy in human nature. The artist's love of beauty and creative spirit are housed in the right hemisphere, they said, and the scientist's intellect in the left.

So, it was at this point that the findings began to skew into the popular notions of right-brain and left-brain thinking. This distortion also reflects Western culture, which emphasizes and rewards almost exclusively the more linear, analytical way of thinking. And as such, it should be no surprise that the left hemisphere, with its language abilities and rational, linear skill-set was "found" to be the dominant force in the

We drew pictures before we wrote words. Ancient Anasazi pictographs from the Canyon de Chelly in northeastern Arizona. Courtesy of the National Park Service.

On May 18, 1980, Lawrence Hudetz photographed a moment in time–a face–and as the story goes, suggested this image could be The Face of Loo-Wit, legendary female spirit of Mount St. Helens. Courtesy of Lawrence Hudetz.

Cyclonic storm 1,200 miles north of
Hawaii photographed from Apollo
9. This complex adaptive system
models the business environment.
Courtesy of NASA.

Shots are heard around the world.
banner hung on a busy street corner
in Bratislava, Czechoslovakia (now
lovakia) in June 1990 commemorates
e one-year anniversary of the student
revolt in Tiannamen Square.
Photographed by Irene Sanders

The nonlinear aspects of nature, seen here in the branches of a tree, are helping us to appreciate the nonlinear realities of the business environment. Courtesy of the National Park Service.

Does a fern look like a mountain? Fractal geometry helps us see relationships where in the past we saw none. Courtesy of the National Park Service.

The Himalayas as seen from space. Courtesy of NASA.

You can't measure a coastline with a ruler, nor can you understand today's business environment with quantitative tools alone. Oregon coast. Courtesy of Lawrence Hudetz.

Can you identify the fractal qualities in this picture? A small garden area just inside the entrance to the forum in Rome, Italy. Courtesy of L.L. Griffin.

Does this look familiar? Or ha
this perspective fooled you? E:
rising as seen from the surface
the moon. Courtesy of NASA.

Our ultimate challenge is understanding this complex adaptive system. Courtesy
of NASA.

brain's important work as reflected in the researchers' witticism "Don't leave home without your left hemisphere."

From this perspective, then, the split-brain research began to find its way into popular psychology. Because each of us has a well-developed set of skills, which conform generally to the description of one of the two hemispheres, the research seemed to identify and affirm our individual strengths. But instead of realizing that a healthy brain functions as a whole and asking how we might better develop and utilize the functions of both hemispheres, we began to identify ourselves as one or the other.

We described left-brain thinkers as articulate, logical, and well-organized, while right-brained individuals were artistic, intuitive, and not really "thinkers" at all. We began to view the "other" as wrong or severely limited, and this myth has been hard to dispel.

Fortunately, current scientific research is directing us away from this dualistic perspective and toward a more complete view of whole-brain functioning. Although we do seem to have an innate preference for one set of skills over the other, we use both. Otherwise, we'd have a hard time finding the words to express an idea or the right paint for the porch.

The brain is enormously complex and much is still unknown, but scientists now believe that it operates like a bioelectrical network, making connections wherever needed to perform a task. They also believe that there are systems that mediate between and among the brain's highly specialized and more subtle functions. In addition to the brain's role in regulating our vital physiology, questions about brain-mind interaction and consciousness are among the most hotly debated topics in neuroscience today.[4]

Among neuroscientists it is generally agreed that the term "mind" refers to "a collection of mental processes" such as thoughts, feelings, memory, and learning. And the brain is the organ that supports mental activity. With these definitions to guide us, it's obvious that our mind is much more than the sum of the brain's geographically based capacities. In these distinctions we find a way through the right-brain, left-brain dilemma and clues to the real source of creativity and insight.

Like a spark of lightning that finds a path through the night sky, our brain-mind interactions create unique patterns of electrical connectivity. Some are localized, like a bolt of lightning hurled to the ground, while others light up the horizon like fireworks, through broad complex patterns of interaction.

New scientific research corroborates well-known stories about moments of intuition, insight, and exceptional creativity. Literally and figuratively these experiences light up our internal horizon by engaging and integrating capacities from both hemispheres.

> Generally speaking, the germ of a future composition comes suddenly and unexpectedly. . . . It takes root with extraordinary force and rapidity, shoots up through the earth, puts forth branches and leaves, and finally blossoms. . . . I forget everything and behave like a mad man; everything within me starts pulsing and quivering; hardly have I begun to sketch, ere one thought follows another.[5]
>
> ——Tchaikovsky

The word insight implies "seeing into," penetrating or understanding something previously hidden or oblique, an elucidating glimpse. Stories and studies about moments of insight provide this list of common characteristics:[6]

- It comes after intense preparation or study of the problem to which it responds.
- It comes in a "flash" while conscious thought is focused elsewhere.
- It may be contrary to the direction you have been pursuing on the problem.

- It enters consciousness fully formed. In this sense it is global. Instead of answering a specific question, the answer is revealed through its relationship to the whole: a painter sees his finished creation; a musician hears the entire composition; and a mathematician understands how years of work fit together.
- It is accompanied by a heightened state of awareness. The immediate surroundings appear more vivid, and you may experience a rush of emotion such as anxiety, excitement, or gratitude.
- There is an intuitive certainty about its correctness.
- The "truth" of it is supported by an aesthetic knowing. It appeals to one's sense of beauty and craftsmanship. There is an elegance or gracefulness to the insight. It is consistent or harmonious with what is already known about the problem, and it will most assuredly withstand the rigors of critique.

These descriptions represent the right-hemisphere strengths of intuitive knowing, wholeness, and beauty, but they are linked inextricably to the process of reasoning or an understanding of the significance and use of the insight. And of course, the insight would be meaningless to anyone else without the ability to recall and express it both verbally and in writing.

Central to the concept of insight is its relationship to the unconscious or preintellectual mind. The list of characteristics above tells us that an insight forms while the "conscious mind is focused elsewhere" and makes itself known in a "flash" of conscious recognition.

Much is unknown about the unconscious mind. I like to think of it as a Cuisinart or a blender, holding and swirling together a lifetime of experiences, thoughts, memories, information, images, and associations. It's always on, taking in more food for thought.

Sometimes I intentionally search through it, hoping to recall a memory or make an association to help me solve a problem. At other times it makes the connection for me and offers it up like a gift. It is from this field of unconscious, preintellectual activity that our insights spring forth into conscious awareness.

Jules-Henri Poincaré, a brilliant French mathematician of the late nineteenth and early twentieth centuries, describes an experience in which he had reached an impasse in his work and turned his attention elsewhere, only to have the answer appear unexpectedly. His story illustrates the mysterious role of the unconscious mind and captures the essence of the perceptive moment.

> I left Caen, where I was living, to go on a geologic excursion under the auspices of the School of Mines. The incidents to travel made me forget my mathematical work. Having reached Coutances, we entered an omnibus to go to some place or other. At the moment I put my foot on the step, the idea came to me, without anything in my former thoughts seeming to have paved the way for it. . . . I did not verify the idea; I should not have had time, as upon taking my seat in the omnibus, I went on with a conversation already commenced, but I felt perfect certainty. On my return to Caen, for convenience sake, I verified the result at my leisure.[7]

This story and the stories of others who have experienced a sudden illumination have another characteristic in common: *The insight always seems to come as a surprise. It catches the recipient off guard.*

In this next section we'll begin to explore ways in which we can encourage the process of insight. While I don't believe that we can invoke insight, I do believe we can stimulate it through the use of visual thinking.

When we compare the stories of those who receive spontaneous insights with those who are known to be visual thinkers, there are some revealing similarities. Both use the capabilities of the whole brain: There are qualitative and quantitative aspects to their revelations. But the insight is experienced and expressed through the right-hemisphere qualities of beauty, its relationship to the whole, and an intuitive knowing about its correctness even before it is critiqued.

And for both, imagery plays a central role. Insights often come into consciousness through the mind's eye in the form of images or symbols, including musical notes, mathematical equations, and dreamtime metaphors.

> Straightway the ideas flow in upon me, directly from God, and not only do I see distinct themes in my mind's eye, but they are clothed in the right forms, harmonies, and orchestration. Measure by measure the finished product is revealed to me when I am in those rare, inspired moods . . . a condition when the conscious mind is in abeyance and the subconscious is in control, for it is through the subconscious mind, which is part of Omnipotence, that inspiration comes.
>
> —Johannes Brahms[8]

The biggest difference between those who receive spontaneous insights and those who are known to be visual thinkers is that visual thinkers consciously nurture the process of insight. They use their imaginations to engage both intuition and intellect.

Just as Einstein rode an imaginary beam of light, a visual thinker will create a picture or model of the problem in their mind, play with it, move it around, work with it, refine it, and use it to raise more questions. They often draw or make models to push their thinking further. In other words, they are quite adept at using various imaginative and graphic approaches to give concrete form to abstract ideas.

> It is absolutely immaterial to me whether I run my turbine in thought or test it in my shop. I even note if it is out of balance. There is no difference whatever, the results are the same. In this

way I am able to rapidly develop and perfect a conception without touching anything. When I have gone as far as to embody in the invention every possible improvement I can think of and see not fault anywhere, I put into concrete form this final product of my brain.

—Nikola Tesla,[9]

inventor of the alternating-current generator
and power transmission system

Through this process they stimulate and integrate dissimilar but complementary brain-mind processes, which allow them to explore and develop new concepts. For a visual thinker, the ability to see and interact with a problem or question is the key to insight. *Visual images activate the deeper levels of awareness and engage the unconscious pre-intellectual mind.*

As humans we are sentient beings whose primary sense is vision. Our brains are stimulated more by visual cues than by any of our other senses. From birth to death, we interpret the world through visual images. So, the idea of using visual perception as a means of analysis is absolutely natural. We've been doing it since the dawn of humankind.

One of the most intriguing aspects of our visual mind is its ability to recognize patterns, similarities and relationships among two or more things. We recognize patterns in faces, textiles, architecture, charts, graphs, and even in political rhetoric and world events. And we are capable of pattern recognition even when the pattern is broken, incomplete, or asymmetrical.

Even though pattern recognition is part of our daily experience, much is still unknown about how it actually works. But we do know that it helps the mind make the connections that give birth to new ideas and innovations. Until recently, however, we have not known how to engage this power *intentionally* for the purpose of promoting insight.

Now, for the first time in history, we have the knowledge, the tools and techniques, and the sense of urgency to develop visual thinking as the essential *insight-foresight* skill of the future. In addition to information from neuroscience about brain-mind interaction, the fields of art and psychology are helping us understand the role of imagery in the creative process. And now, the new field of *scientific visualization* is bringing all of this information together by using computer graphics to demonstrate how visual images can be used to engage our imaginations and enhance learning.

Pattern recognition is an extremely complex mental process, and one which computers can only duplicate in a rudimentary way. So, in an interesting twist away from our usual passive reliance on the computer to do it for us, we are now learning how to use the computer to teach ourselves how to do it better.

Scientific visualization is *the* art *of making the unseen visible*[10] through the integration of high-speed computation and colorful 3-D graphics. In the past scientists were stuck, literally, for months or years trying to understand the world through mathematical models. Now computers can translate numbers into pictures, creating numerically based *visual models* that tap the researcher's powers of visual perception.

In his book *Visualization: The Second Computer Revolution*, Richard Mark Freidhoff explains,

> Our ability to recognize a pattern, or to make a comparison, in numerical data does not compare with the eye/brain's fantastic ability to recognize and compare graphic forms . . . visualization eliminates the computational barrier in favor of visual thinking. . . . Much of the information processing required to solve a problem is moved from conscious intellection to the preconscious processes of the visual system.[11]

The interactivity of scientific visualization is also an important aspect in the discovery process, as it is described by Jean-Francois Colonna in *Frontiers of Scientific Visualization:*

[P]ictures intended as little more than an efficient method for presenting a vast amount of data can be a means of discovery, used to discern the unexpected or to observe something that no physical instrument can show. . . . Like the various components of a musical orchestra which all come together to create a useful whole, the scientist, numerical calculation, and picture synthesis all work together to form a scientific instrument.[12]

Researchers are able to change variables, add new ones, and watch the results take shape. The interactivity allows them to develop new ideas and questions, to follow their intuition and use their imaginations.

Visualization, Colonna says, has many uses. The list below, with a few amplifications, could easily describe the insight-foresight requirements needed in today's business world.

- Synthesis
- Comparison or Validation of Data
- Detecting Changes
- Comprehending Abstract Concepts
- Seeing Inaccessible or Invisible Phenomena and Relationships
- Communications
- Discovery[13]

Visual thinking is finally coming out of the minds of the fortunate few and into the mainstream. And as it does, let's look at some familiar examples.

Physicians and other health care professionals have been using pictures and computer graphics to interpret physical data for years. From X rays, to the peaks and valleys on a basic electrocardiogram, to the sophisticated and colorful pictures generated by various scanning and imaging devices, visual thinking (although they don't call it that) is an integral part of our health care system.

Computer-aided design (CAD) is a great help to architects in developing and revising building plans. And the Doppler radar screen on the evening news helps us understand our local weather and keeps us up-to-date on weather patterns across the country.

Now, computers and graphics software are everywhere: in our homes, schools, offices, and in some cases even the local espresso bar. Today, interactive technology and computer graphics are widespread, giving us opportunities to increase our visual skills.

This rapid shift to visual modes of thinking and analysis is an historical turning point that coincides with science's exploration of chaos theory and complexity. Remember as we discussed in Chapter 2, chaos theory and complexity describe the behavior of nonlinear systems that move, grow, or change.

In these systems the variables are changing and interacting with each other constantly, so the underlying pattern, shape, or structure is only observable over time. For scientists, the ability to visualize the behavior of a nonlinear system over time was the key to understanding the system's underlying dynamics. The pictures allowed them to engage both intellect and intuition, as described by James Gleick in *Chaos: Making a New Science.*

> To chaos researchers, mathematics has become an experimental science, with the computer replacing laboratories full of test tubes and microscopes. Graphic images are the key. "It's masochism for a mathematician to do without pictures," one chaos specialist would say. "How can they see the relationship between that motion and this? How can they develop intuition?"[14]

The Lorenz Attractor was the first *picture* of a nonlinear dynamical system. Until then, scientists had not been able to see the order hidden within disorder.

> For years, no single object would inspire more illustrations, even motion pictures, than the mysterious curve depicted at the end, the double spiral that became known as the Lorenz attractor. For the first time, Lorenz's pictures had shown what it meant to say, "This is complicated." All the richness of chaos was there.[15]

Scientific visualization is the use of computer graphics to study quantitative data and numerical information. As we have just heard, it is a tremendous asset to scientists. But mathematics and numerical simulations cannot provide the insight nor the foresight we need to understand the behavior of sociopolitical systems. The field of scientific visualization has, however, demonstrated how we can use *visual models* to stimulate both by engaging the enormous information-processing abilities of the visual mind.

Our challenge now is finding a way to engage our visual processing abilities to see and understand the multiple complexities—the unseen relationships, connections, and patterns of interaction—that are creating the dynamics of the real world in which our decisions are being made.

In order to do that, we'll venture into the woods and take a path that few have yet to find. But first, I want to summarize the key points—the stepping-stones—that have helped us get this far.

1. We are a visual society, yet there are some things we just don't see.
2. The primary reason for this is that we don't know how to see or visualize the multiple complexities—relationships, connections, patterns of interaction, and subtle changes—that are creating the *dynamics* of the real world context in which our decisions are being made.
3. Only the human mind is capable of dealing with the level of complexity in today's world.
4. Visual thinking is the key to *insight* and *foresight*.

5. Insight and foresight are stimulated by engaging the powers of intuition and intellect through the use of visual images.

6. Visual images activate the deeper levels of awareness and engage the unconscious, preintellectual mind.

7. Through our visual system the unconscious, preintellectual mind is capable of pattern recognition. It sees and understands relationships and connections much quicker than our intellectual, analytical mind.

8. The rapid shift to visual modes of thinking and analysis coincided with the exploration of chaos theory and complexity.

9. For scientists, the ability to visualize the behavior of a nonlinear system was the key to understanding chaos theory and complexity. Once they were able to see the behavior of a nonlinear system, they were able to think about and explore the world in new ways.

10. Because the sociopolitical world is made up of complex adaptive systems that are constantly moving and changing, organizations have the same need to see and think about their environment in new ways. The old quantitative methods are not enough.

11. In order to do this we must connect the clues provided in the information above.

In order to see the future as it is emerging, we need a visual tool that will engage both our intuition and our intellect. We need a way to see and understand the underlying relationships, connections, and patterns of interaction that are creating the *dynamics* of the real world context in which our decisions are being made.

In order to find this perspective, we'll go to a place I've been exploring. What I'll show you is a way to use your perceptual abilities to understand the world around you more fully.

■ ■ ■

Yet it often happens that we do not see what is quite near at hand and clear. And we have a clear example of this right before us. For everything that was demonstrated and explained to us so laboriously, is shown to us by Nature so openly and clearly that nothing could be plainer or more obvious.

—Galileo

Galileo at Work

During most of the twelve years that I worked in Washington, DC, I kept a small apartment in the city, but spent as much time as possible at my wonderful old farmhouse in Harpers Ferry, WV, about 60 miles northwest of the District. I've always been an early riser, so it wasn't unusual for me to catch the 5:55 A.M. train to Washington. With a cup of coffee and the *Washington Post,* I'd start the seventy-five-minute ride through the countryside and into Union Station.

What I remember most about those morning rides is the internal shift I felt as gentle pastoral settings gave way to suburban congestion and, finally, to the frenetic pace of the nation's capital. An internal shift also occurred in the evening as I returned to the quiet beauty of the country, with views of the Potomac River and a palette of colors that changed with the seasons.

I've always liked the contrast between the country and the city. One stimulates my senses and the other my mind. Both are a part of me and neither would willingly be sacrificed for the other.

As I began to search for ways to integrate the findings from chaos theory and complexity into my strategic thinking and planning work with organizations, I realized that the internal shifts I felt on those morning and evening train rides were prompted by the visual transition from natural landscapes to cityscapes and back again. I began to experiment in my mind with various juxtapositions, just to see what new thoughts and ideas I might have.

What did nature have to teach us about the sociopolitical world? Could I use juxtaposed images to help my clients understand the tangles, connections, and changes that characterized their business environment? These ideas and questions swirled around in my internal blender for a while, and finally they began to gel.

Most popular books on chaos theory and complexity include beautiful photographs of canyons, forests, ferns, and coastlines, all there to illustrate the complex, irregular, and changeable architecture of nature. These pictures show us the *fractal* qualities of nature.

The term "fractal" was coined in 1975 by mathematician Benoit Mandelbrot to describe a new concept in geometry. Classical Euclidean geometry, the kind we were all taught in school, uses linear abstract concepts like cones, spheres, and lines to describe the natural world. Yet, when you look into a forest, across a rolling landscape, up through the trees in a city park, or down at the leaves under your feet, you see that the real world is filled with a variety of rich colors, shapes, patterns, and textures.

Mandelbrot, like other chaos and complexity pioneers, had been searching for new concepts and tools with which to study the real nature of Nature. In *The Fractal Geometry of Nature* he describes his frustration with standard geometry:

> I claim that many patterns of Nature are so irregular and fragmented, that compared to Euclid—a term used in this work to denote all standard geometry—Nature exhibits not simply a higher degree of but an altogether different level of complexity. . . . The existence of these patterns challenges us to study those forms which Euclid leaves aside as being "formless" to investigate the morphology of the "amorphous." Mathematicians have disdained this challenge, however, and have increasingly chosen to flee from nature by devising theories unrelated to anything we can see or feel.[16]

As a mathematician, Mandelbrot's new geometry is statistically based. But the term *fractal* represents a major breakthrough in helping mathematicians and nonmathematicians alike see and understand the world as it really is. The word fractal is derived from the Latin word *fractus*, meaning fragmented or irregular. Geometry means literally to measure the Earth. So fractal geometry is a method for measuring the irregular, fragmented, nonlinear aspects of the Earth, i.e., nature.

Fractal geometry is much more closely related to the *look* and *feel* of the real world. It recognizes an order found within the irregular aspects of nature. It's an order, which in the past we have not seen, because in a sense we didn't know how to see it. It doesn't fit the classical linear definition of order. The fractal concept helps us appreciate the orderly yet constantly changing world in which we live.

It has become popular to use the word fractal as a noun rather than as an adjective. People frequently ask me, "What is *a* fractal?" This is just as awkward as asking, "What is a red?" The word fractal is an adjective describing the qualities or characteristics of being broken, fragmented, irregular, or rough. So, the more appropriate question is "What is fractal?" What is irregular or fragmented but orderly at the same time?

There are two general characteristics that help us recognize this new type of order. *Fractal forms are self-similar.* Like ferns in a forest, bark on a tree, or the lines on our faces, patterns and shapes are repeated. Something in each new impression is familiar, a reflection of previous patterns and shapes. Look into the center of a flower, study a blade of grass or the underside of a leaf, and you'll see the self-similar patterns.

Fractal forms are self-similar across scales. Patterns and shapes are repeated in finer and finer detail. Pick up a moss-covered rock and recognize the shape of a mountain. Look at an image of the human circulatory system and you'll see the branching pattern of a river or stream. Look into the bark of an old oak tree, see the similarity in the layers underneath, and you'll recognize the shape and texture of a forest.

Hollywood uses fractal technology to make movie magic. A rock becomes a mountain, a scattering of wildflowers turns into a sea of color, a few head of cattle are transformed into a stampeding herd, and a slice of Manhattan expands into a full unbroken skyline.

The concept of self-similarity across scales has also given us new ways to appreciate the special appeal of art and architecture. Patterns and shapes that are repeated in finer and finer detail add depth, texture, and a rich coherence to paintings and structures. The old European cathedrals are wonderful examples of self-similarity across scales, as are the paintings of Monet and Van Gogh.

There is an aesthetically pleasing quality to fractal forms in nature as they come together to create a beautiful whole. We respond positively to scenes where the buildings and landscape share a fractal quality. Frank Lloyd Wright had an intuitive feel for this concept, as do others who work to integrate their designs with nature.

On the other hand, each of us could cite an example of a building where the fractal quality is missing. My favorite "worst" is a building just outside of Washington, DC, near Dulles International Airport. From a distance, this building looks like an upside down black triangle; large at the top and tapering down to the ground. The sight of this building rising out of the treetops is almost ominous. There is no sense of coherence between the building and its natural surroundings. There is no fractal quality to the whole scene.

One of the most interesting aspects of fractal forms is their interface with change. Mandelbrot uses the example of a coastline to illustrate this point. We are used to thinking of coastlines as static, maplike in their dependability.

Imagine that you're standing barefoot in the water watching the waves splash up against a rocky shore. You get a little closer, and suddenly you're aware that every wave leaves an impression. You see the sand and small pebbles being dragged and tossed with each wave. And you may not be able to see it, but you know that each wave carves the larger rocks, a mini–Grand Canyon forming as you watch. If you extend your imagination into the future, you'll see that the coastline is actually getting longer, as the splashing erodes, reshapes, and extends the visible boundary.

Fractal forms are found at the boundaries between matter that already exists, like a coastline, and the motion of external elements or forces against it, like the waves. The fractal qualities of nature are evidence that we are part of, not separate from, a world of process, motion, and change. The concept of fractals contributed to the recognition that nature is both orderly and infinitely creative. As in the wistful tracings of wind across a sand dune, something constant moves forward through chaos.

The idea of fractals helps us see patterns and shapes where in the past we saw nothing distinct or dismissed what we did see as insignificant. Now we have a way to see the world anew.

Take a walk in the woods or through a park and see how many shapes and patterns you notice. Let your eye scan the area and find a place that interests you. Your eye will find the patterns before your mind can recognize them. Pay attention to the layering of patterns such as pine cones, pine needles, leaves, bark, branches, and vines. Step back and see the whole picture. Each tree, flower, plant, or rock has its own fractal qualities, but together they create a rich web of connections. The patterns and shapes work together to create a coherent and orderly whole.

And that's the important point for our purposes. This tangle of patterns, shapes, connections, and relationships in nature is a powerful metaphor for the nonlinear sociopolitical world. It helps us develop intuition about the web of interrelationships in the world around us.

Hold that picture in your mind and ask yourself, "How might this way of seeing the world help me understand the business environment? How might these concepts and ideas be useful in other areas of my life?" In your mind begin to see that the business environment is created and continuously reshaped by a vast network of connections, relationships, and patterns of interaction.

SUGGESTIONS FOR ENHANCING VISUAL THINKING

- *Draw a picture.* Learn to use a pen and paper as an extension of your mind. Think about a question, issue, or problem on which you are working. If you were to draw a picture of it, what would it look like? Take a pen and begin creating a picture or an image of the situation. Use your own questions, thoughts, and imagination to guide your drawing and push your understanding forward. Stay with it, even if you feel that nothing is happening. Keep your pad nearby while you work on something else. You may be surprised by the insights or new thoughts that begin to break through. The *campfires of thought* image found in Chapter 1 was developed using this technique.

- *Notice those things to which you are paying attention.* For example, Don Burke, a physician whose specialty is tropical infectious diseases, told me a story about walking along a beach in Thailand and realizing that he was focusing on the rivulets or small channels carved in the sand by the movement of the ocean water washing over it and then receding. What he noticed was that once a channel started to form, the water found it again and again, and the channel grew larger or developed branches as the water repeatedly washed over and filled it up. He made a connection between what he was observing and a research question on which he was working.

  He saw the rivulets as a metaphor for the path of a virus through a population. This led him to develop a new theory about how a virus gets a foothold in a population and creates a channel through which other viruses can move. Noticing what he was paying attention to helped him visualize and then theorize about the dynamics of some of the world's most deadly diseases.

- *Use a metaphor and its metaphorm[17] to develop your understanding.* A metaphor is a statement or an image in which you compare or connect one thing with another, such as "negotiating this business deal feels like trying to find my way through a forest at midnight without a flashlight" or "loving you is like a hot cup of coffee on a cold winter morning." A simple phrase or image is used to explain something more complex.

A meta*phorm* as defined by Todd Siler in his book *Think Like a Genius* creates a deeper level of understanding, by exploring more fully the comparison and its connections to the real life situation or question you are hoping to understand. For example, in what ways is a cup of coffee on a cold winter morning like my feelings of love for you? What are the similarities between how that cup of coffee smells, looks, feels, tastes, fills me up, and takes the chill off a cold winter morning, and my feelings of love for you? Is that cup of coffee (à la you) a welcomed and familiar friend? Do I look forward to that familiar greeting each morning? Am I satisfied (with my cup of coffee/you) or is the anticipation more exciting than the actual experience?

In other words, a metaphorm will help you develop an image in your mind and then explore it. This type of associative exercise will help you develop the skill of visual thinking by giving you images with which to work. It will show you how to strengthen your mind's eye, leading to greater insight and creativity.

So, practice. Pick a topic and begin. You may have to try several metaphors before you find the one that feels right. Once you have the comparison statement in mind, go deeper. See the comparison in your mind or draw a picture to help you visualize the connections.

Go on and develop the metaphorm; fill out the comparison and its real life connections. Push yourself to make as many connections as possible. And don't automatically dismiss those that seem outrageous—they may be your most valuable.

In business the "sky" is a bewildering unruly interconnected universe of people, data, and events. Because the issues and challenges that any business will face in the future are perking in its environment today, it is crucial to find ways to see and organize that information now.

With the technique of *environmental scanning* and the use of a *FutureScape*™, we now have a way to see that sky, with its unique patterns, dynamics, and cloud formations. We have a way to see change or rain coming—in time for you to fill your trunk with umbrellas and make some money!

Whether it's the likelihood of rain during tomorrow afternoon's baseball game, college funds for the children, a retirement home, or our business, it's the future that every individual and organization wants to plan for. But seeing into the future is not a skill most of us have developed. It's a murky area filled with suspicion, gimmickry, and foreboding.

For example, each New Year's Eve brings a series of articles reviewing the events of the year just past and making predictions about the year ahead. Articles about the future are usually illustrated with cartoons showing a gypsy looking into a crystal ball or someone looking into the distance through a pair of binoculars. The caption under the cartoon invariably makes fun of what the seer sees or of the whole effort in general.

Cartoons like this convey the three major beliefs that most people have about the future. One, the future is located somewhere far away from today. Two, someone else must look and interpret it for us. And three, the future is not really ours to know anyway.

What these three beliefs have in common is an underlying sense of being disconnected from the future, an uncertainty about what's to come, and a desire to control what seems uncontrollable. All this leads us to a variety of behaviors—denial, avoidance, compulsion—designed to give us some measure of control over the future.

At a meeting in Dallas a few years ago, I heard the president of a large training and consulting firm tell an audience about his first flight from New York to London aboard the Concorde. He described being startled as he looked out the window to see a huge wall of darkness moving toward him with great speed. What he actually observed was a reflection of the Concorde approaching nightfall somewhere over the Atlantic at a speed of Mach 2. Nevertheless, he used this image as a metaphor for the future and concluded his remarks by urging the audience to "attack the future, before it overwhelms you."

It's not the future we need to attack, but rather our fear of the unknown, looming before us like a wall of darkness. We need a way to break through the feeling that we are hurtling toward the future along a trajectory of change, unable to avoid a collision and with no hope of rescue.

That the future will be different from today is a given. What we struggle with is our desire to know how it will be different and what we can do to influence it.

Forecasting, the most familiar tool for getting advance information about the future, is based on analysis of existing conditions and trends. Through analysis and the use of mathematical models, forecasters estimate or calculate a future state. Classical forecasting models are based on the old cause-effect belief that, given a set of initial conditions, all you have to do is project those forward and arrive at a conclusion about the future.

Because the margin of error is large enough in many of the questions tackled—economic conditions, mortality rates, or the motion of planets—forecasters seem to hit the mark often enough to get our attention. But when the techniques of forecasting are applied to more complex questions such as politics, retail profits, or the price of petroleum, the success rates drop dramatically.

5

FROM FORECASTING TO FORESIGHT

What's the weather gonna do? is a question asked by ninnies.
The answer to this question is obvious. It'll do what it damn
well pleases when it pleases. . . . It has better things to do.
Storms to brew, winds to whirl, that sort of thing. Not that the
weather doesn't occasionally listen in. It eavesdrops on the mil-
lions of forecasts transmitted daily and in a low, hearty rumble,
laughs.

—NIKE ADVERTISEMENT
EcoTraveler Magazine

From Bombay to Boston, around the world and back to Bombay, the
skies are connected. Yet most of us are only concerned about what's
happening in the sky over our own heads. We forget or never think
about the fact that the weather we experience is part of one vast interconnected system that encircles the Earth. On this planet, which is
three-quarters water, we are all tied together through layers of swirling,
colliding, and constantly changing levels of moisture and heat.

The challenge for meteorologists in coming anywhere close to forecasting the local weather is to see and understand the dynamics of the
larger system in a coherent and realistic way. The same thing is true in
the business world.

The reason for this, as we know from the new science, is that in complex adaptive systems change can be introduced at almost any point. Through the Butterfly Effect any change in initial conditions can create dramatic changes in the future.

There are so many interacting factors that contribute to the outcome of a political campaign, the preferences and purchasing ability of retail customers, and the international politics of petroleum that it would be almost impossible to make a prediction about the future based on any one set of initial conditions. And at some level, politics, retail profits, and petroleum are all interconnected.

Foresight, on the other hand, is the ability to *see* what is *emerging*—to understand the dynamics of the larger context and to recognize new *initial conditions* as they are forming. In today's complex and rapidly changing world, the development of foresight skills is a must. Without foresight, all we can see ahead of us is a wall of darkness. With foresight, we see the future as it is taking shape.

Our ability to think and act with foresight has been enhanced by rapid advances in technology and telecommunications. Real time information floods our homes and offices. We have immediate access to news and information from around the world. Through our new understanding about the dynamics of change in a world made up of complex adaptive systems, we know that the present is also the future. Whatever is happening today is shaping tomorrow.

Many of my speaking engagements are scheduled around meals. So, to illustrate the relationship between the present and the future, I point out that "those of you who ate the sweet rolls or dessert will know that the future is happening today, when they show up on your hips a few days from now." Acting with foresight in this situation would mean not eating the sweets, cutting back on other foods, or exercising to burn the extra calories.

With foresight, we have the ability to influence the future by *responding* to and *influencing* what is *emerging*. With foresight we can see change coming and respond—before a crisis arises. We have an opportunity to focus our resources in ways that will begin to influence the future immediately. Until now, however, what has been missing in our attempts at foresight is the *sight* part of the process.

When I ask my friends and clients what they see or envision when they think of Internet and the World Wide Web, they usually answer quickly. They imagine a giant spider web or layers of interconnected spider webs surrounding the Earth. The words, World Wide Web, provide an image, as do the illustrations used to advertise various web search engines.

When I ask the same people how they see or envision the environment in which their businesses operate, they hesitate, searching for words, images, and concepts. When pushed, they use words like "mess," "volatile," and "chaotic," but no image or picture comes to mind.

In my work, the challenge is always to help individuals and organizations make the best decisions possible. In the mid-1980s I began experimenting with a variety of visual techniques to help individuals and organizations *see* and *understand* the environment or context in which their decisions were being made. I wanted to find a way to help them expand their thinking about the world, the future, and the changes affecting their businesses. And I wanted to help them see the environment in real time, as it is today, not as it was last month or last year.

The concept of *environmental scanning*—the process of gathering information about changes in the environment of a business or industry—provided the framework for developing my approach to *thinking* about change. And, chaos theory and complexity provided the *understanding* about the dynamics of change. Together they helped me develop a technique for *seeing* and interpreting the dynamics of the larger system or environment. This is done by creating a *FutureScape*™, an artistic representation of all the factors impacting or influencing the business, issue or question being considered. On pages 114–120, I'll show you how to create a FutureScape™.

Whether we are aware of it or not, we are constantly scanning our environment. Because we take in information through all our senses, most of us are not aware of how much information we have access to each day. We may not call it scanning, but we are overloaded with information.

Unless you have completely isolated yourself, you can't help but know something about what's happening in the world. I am always amazed at the bits and pieces of news and information that float in and out the door of my local coffeeshop each morning. *The Ground Up* is the best place I can think of to get an instant update or an opinion on just about any subject.

Fishing or casting a wide net to see what turns up are both good metaphors for *purposeful* scanning. When I'm traveling on business, I scan by reading everything I can get my hands on. What I'm usually scanning for is a sense of the most current issues and events, and then a sense of the relationships and connections among them. Because I work across many industries, this type of information helps me facilitate the efforts of my clients to think beyond their immediate concerns.

Our ability to receive, process, and incorporate new information has created a global environment that is in effect one vast system with many interconnecting points. In this complex global system, change can be introduced at almost any point. The challenge, therefore, in decision-making is to find a way to see and understand the global system in a realistic and coherent way. A *FutureScape*™ helps to provide that global perspective.

Often, when teaching the process of scanning in Washington, DC, I take my class to the National Air and Space Museum to see the movie *The Blue Planet*. In this film the Earth is observed from space through footage taken by various space shuttle missions. Through the magic of IMAX and the enormous 50-foot-by-75-foot screen, we feel as if we are in the shuttle looking back at our beautiful blue planet, spinning gently against the dark backdrop of space. From this perspective we observe Earth's constantly changing environment, we appreciate the interconnected ecosystem shared by all life on Earth, and we see how the careless actions of man are disrupting the global balance on which we all depend.

This film, seen in this setting, provides a rich and intense experience in scanning from a global perspective. And on those occasions when my class includes managers from other parts of the world, it creates a sense of unity and shared responsibility that transcends religion, culture, and politics.

The first step, then, in environmental scanning is to understand the importance of stepping back in your mind's eye and observing your business, issue, or question from a global perspective. A FutureScape™ is created by mapping the environment from this larger perspective. The purpose of mapping is to create as accurate a representation as possible of the global environment in which your business operates or in which your issue or question must be considered. The map includes all the factors affecting or potentially affecting the subject you are studying.

The map becomes a FutureScape™ only in its totality—and after you step back and observe the whole scene. In a FutureScape™, as in a landscape or an oceanscape, the details become important only through their participation in the overall picture. Each detail contributes to the whole, but the significance of each detail can only be appreciated through the qualities of the whole scene.

There are two major differences, however, between a FutureScape™ and landscape. First, through the process of visual thinking and the application of your new knowledge about the process of change in complex adaptive systems, a FutureScape™ becomes a moving, evolving, organically complex whole, that is being shaped and reshaped through its constantly changing field of connections, relationships, and patterns of interaction. And the significance of specific details or data may change as the overall environment changes.

A FutureScape™ supports the process of visual thinking by helping you link your intuitive sense of events in the larger environment with what you already know and what the data indicate. This visual synthesis promotes insight about the present and foresight about the future—the keys to successful strategic thinking.

Following are the steps for creating a FutureScape™. By yourself or with a partner, practice making your own map. After you get comfortable with the mapping process, then you'll be able to use it with a larger group, which is how it's actually used in a strategic thinking and planning session.

CREATING A FUTURESCAPE™
(Read steps 1–10 before starting.)

1. *Identify the business, question, or situation you want to map and describe it to your partner.* This will allow your partner to ask you questions and coach you through the process.

2. *Make sure you have a variety of colored markers and some masking tape.* I prefer water-based markers over permanent markers, because they will not ruin your clothes. *Save the black marker for step number 10.*

3. *On a large sheet of paper, draw an ellipse in the center.* I prefer an ellipse instead of a circle because it prompts the eye to see a horizon and because it helps the mind shift out of its comfortable linear mode. Use a large sheet of easel or flip-chart paper. Hang it on the wall with masking tape.

4. *In the center of the ellipse, write the name of the business, question, or situation you want to scan.* Name the map. This will help keep you focused and will allow any passersby to offer suggestions or ask questions.

A FutureScape™.

5. *Sit in front of the map, if it is your map that is being drawn. The coach stands by the paper, asks questions, and fills in the map.* Sitting in front of your map allows you to see the picture as it is being drawn and to tap into your intuition about what is appearing.

6. *Begin creating the map. Start with the immediate, then go global.* What do you already know about the object of your scanning? What pieces of the puzzle do you see right now? Your coach will help you here. *This is not problem solving. It is a mapping exercise out of which problem solving will be possible. Do not evaluate or make decisions about the words or images that appear in your map. The purpose here is to get what you know out of your head and on paper.*

7. *Don't worry about what goes in or out of the ellipse.* The ellipse represents the immediate or most obvious parts of the environment, so it's the easiest place to begin. The ellipse is designed to help you think about the issue. This is your map, so use it in the way that feels most helpful.

A FutureScape™.

8. *The key to good mapmaking is asking the right questions.* This is where your coach can help. This is why it's important for your coach to understand as much as possible about the issue or question you are scanning. Good listening skills and practice make this easier.

   a. Go back up to step 6. Begin there and then use these questions to help create the map.

   b. Who and what are in the environment? Customers, competitors, new developments, regulation, trends, new technology, politics, global events, etc. Look across industries. What do you see on the horizon?

   c. The questions you ask will depend on the issue or business being considered. Let your knowledge, curiosity, and instincts guide you. What you are trying to do is create a realistic picture of the environment—local, regional, national, and international. Questions for a business in the timber industry, for example, will be different from those in the food or entertainment industries.

d. Let the answers to your questions guide you to another question. For example, when groups of customers are identified, you may feel it important to ask "In what ways is my customer base changing?" What are you hearing from them? Or, How does your competition view you? How do they perceive your strengths?

e. Practice will increase your comfort and skill level with the mapping process.

f. And remember, there will be quiet spaces in the mapping process as you and the participants look at the map and it taps

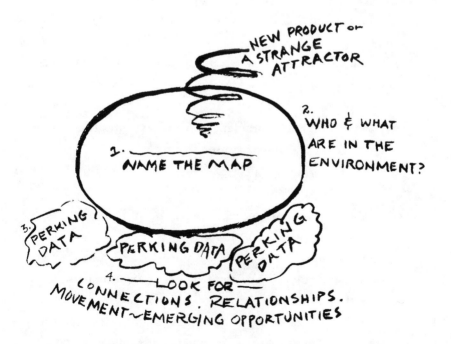

The basic steps in creating a FutureScape™.

your deeper levels of understanding. Stand aside, so everyone can see the map. Ask "What else needs to go up here?" What is missing? What are you thinking about or sensing?

9. *Remember, this map represents the real world, so it should be messy and colorful to emphasize the nonlinear world in which we live and the movement in and around the issue.* It may help if the coach asks the mapmaker what color he or she wants to use and where on the map to place the word or symbol. Most of the time I change colors every time I put something on the map.

The colors are only meant to give the map a sense of depth and movement. There is no other significance, unless the person whose map is being drawn gives it special meaning. *Save the black marker for the next step.*

10. *Identify perking data.* After you have filled in the local and global aspects of your map, ask yourself the following questions. The answers to these questions may already be on the map. If so, circle them in black. If they are not on the map, add them and circle in black.

    a. What seems small now, but if it mushroomed overnight could go through your environment like a bolt of lightning and completely rearrange it?

    b. What could have a dramatic impact on the future of the organization or issue being scanned?

    c. What thoughts or concerns about your work or this issue keep you awake at night?

    d. What is your intuition telling you? What do you feel in your stomach, but don't talk about?

    e. When you drive to work in the morning, and you arrive at the office, but you don't remember how you got there, what were you thinking about on the way in?

    f. What's perking in the environment around this organization or issue? It may not seem like a big concern now, but you know that at some level it's out there.

INTERPRETING THE FUTURESCAPE™

Remember, the future is happening today. The purpose of the mapping process is to allow you to *see, respond to,* and *influence* what is *emerging.*

1. *Begin looking for connections, relationships, and movement in your map.* Do you see relationships or connections that you have not thought of before? How are the elements of your map coming together, clustering, or moving to influence your central issue or question? Let your intuition help you here. What is your sense of the map? What were you thinking, feeling, or sensing as the map was being created? What is the map telling you about your next step related to the central issue or question? Ask your coach to help you. He or she also has a sense of the map that may be very useful.

   This step may feel awkward and that's okay. What you're doing here is beginning the movement from a nonlinear intuitive process into a more linear process. If you can't yet make complete thoughts or sentences out of the map, just jot down words, phrases, or inklings about what the map is telling you. Use a Post-it® pad to capture your ideas. Put each idea on a separate page.

2. *The perking data are your leverage points.* If you are aware of this information at any level, then it is real. The perking data are those new *initial conditions* to which your issue or question is *sensitive.* The perking data are beginning to create the future of your business, issue, or question. If you begin to apply some thinking and planning resources to them *now,* you can influence the outcome.

3. *On another sheet of paper, begin to cluster your Post-it® notes and ideas under general headings.* Out of your clusters a sense of direction will begin to emerge.

A FutureScape™ simulates a live-action weather map. It provides a window to the future and reminds us that change is constant, it cannot be stopped or even slowed down. It helps us *look* beyond the messiness of our everyday experience to *see* the changes affecting our lives and businesses.

Through the map you'll begin to see the connections, relationships, and patterns that are creating the dynamics of the system you're observing. You'll begin to see the creative edge, where the future is emerging. And finally, you will begin to see the leverage points and opportunities for influencing the future.

IMPORTANT ELEMENTS OF THE MAPPING PROCESS

Each element in the mapping process has a purpose and relates to one of the seven principles of strategic thinking as defined by the new science. Let's take a look at how they fit together.

Principle 1: Look at whole systems, not just their parts.

- The ellipse, drawn in the center of the page, symbolizes the importance of stepping back in your mind's eye and scanning the *big-picture context* of the issue or business from a global perspective. It reminds you to see the whole system and its environment—international, national, regional, and local.

Principle 2: There is a relationship between order and disorder, and self-organizing change occurs as a result of their interactions.

- Change occurs as the result of new influences that disrupt existing patterns. Out of these disruptions, new patterns are formed.

- In complex adaptive systems, self-organization occurs as the system creates and responds to changes in itself through a process known as *feedback*. An innovation in one company forces action by another and another, and results in a feedback loop of constant change to which they are all sensitive.

- The new pattern emerges as issues, trends, and technological developments, etc., interact and converge with the deliberate actions taken by affected companies.

- Organizations impacted by an unexpected development often see their situation as a free fall into an abyss. But the process of adaptation reminds us that, although the movement from the old to the new might look and feel chaotic, it represents an opportunity to look at the deeper structures on which the organization has depended. It provides an opportunity to rethink, redirect, reorganize, reposition, and rebuild.

- Using different colors to draw the map without consideration to the organization of ideas or issues creates a sense of depth and movement and simulates the chaotic and complex nature of the overall environment. The challenge is to see or sense where and in what direction the self-organizing changes or new patterns of interaction are emerging. This will help you make decisions about where and how to apply your resources.

Principle 3: A small event in one sector can cause tremendous turbulence in another.

- *The future is happening today.* And it's important to identify perking information about new developments that could impact your business. Look first at your business and industry, and then at other industries, where developments could mushroom overnight and blindside you in the morning. And ask youself what new developments in other disciplines or industries could be of use to you. What changes are beginning to appear on the horizon?

- *These are the emerging initial conditions to which your system may be sensitive.* They are your leverage points. By recognizing your system's initial conditions as they are emerging, you have an opportunity to respond to change before a crisis arises and to influence the future to your advantage.

Principle 4: Maps, models, and visual images make it easier to see connections, relationships, and patterns of interaction.

- Step back and look at your FutureScape™. What do you see or sense about the movement and interaction of the information in your map? The map will help you link your intuition with your intellect through the process of visual thinking.

- Like a large painting hung on a gallery wall, a FutureScape™ will focus the attention of a group out toward their environment. It facilitates systems thinking and allows each participant to bring his or her thoughts, observations, and perspective to the collective act of scanning, or seeing, the big picture.

- Through the mapping process a group will make a *phase transition*. In science a phase transition describes the sudden movement from one state to another, like metal being magnetized or demagnetized, or water changing from a liquid to a gas. The transition takes place when a boundary is crossed and a rapid shift in form takes place. A phase transition is the point of transformation.

  The mapping process helps a group make a phase transition from concrete linear thinking to nonlinear abstract thinking. Because mapping engages the whole brain, it helps a group trust the process long enough for the shift to take place so that important connections can be made.

Principle 5: Scanning across disciplines and industries is the key to seeing emerging conditions, paradigm shifts, and opportunities for innovation.

- The history of chaos theory and complexity is filled with stories about the walls coming down between disciplines. Prior to this, professionals from the different disciplines did not talk to each other and the professional journals of one discipline would not print papers from another.

  But as scientists began to look for connections between different forms of irregularity, the boundaries between disciplines began to open. The questions were too big for any one discipline to answer. This new openness created opportunities for synergistic thinking and cooperative research. Without an overview to guide them, cooperation and sharing of information were the only ways to make sense of the chaos and complexity puzzle.

• Because environmental scanning is both an activity and a state of mind, think about all the ways you receive information: television, radio, the Internet, newspapers, intelligence activities, clients, suppliers, consultants, faculty, and others who interact with your organization. Ask for input from your key stakeholders.

• *But,* most important, remember that the mapping process works best when the participants represent a wide range of disciplines, functions, and perspectives. Together, a diverse group will create a comprehensive and realistic map of the environment.

• Because everyone's perspective is needed and included in the map, and because the emphasis is on understanding changes in the external environment, the process facilitates agreement and buy-in, even from warring factions within an organization. Focusing on the external realities represented in the map shifts the discussion away from who's right or wrong, liberal or conservative, or up or down. The map will *tell* you what's important to pay attention to.

• As an example, the recent epidemic of tuberculosis in New York City could have been prevented or treated at a less expensive stage had public health officials there conducted scanning across boundaries and disciplines.

Many health care providers had seen new cases of TB, but the information had not been brought together to create a coherent "big picture."

Principle 6: Nonlinear thinking is critical to recognizing clues about changes in the environment.

- In *The Mind of the Strategist* Kenichi Ohmae says that "what marks the mind of the strategist is an intellectual elasticity or flexibility that enables him to come up with realistic responses to changing situations, not simply to discriminate with great precision among different shades of gray."[1]

- Because the FutureScape™ engages the whole brain, it taps the nonlinear associative abilities of our brain-mind interactions, which allow us to sense subtle changes and to make connections that would otherwise be missed.

- The use of an artistic representation of an organization's environment—the FutureScape™, the messiness of the final map, the use of colors, the identification of perking information, and the technique of clustering— are all nonlinear features of the overall process.

- Thinking in pictures allows us to link our intuitive sense of events with our intellectual understanding, which stimulates the nonlinear processes of both insight and foresight.

- Intuition alone is not enough, but it is often through our intuitions that the first clues or ideas about a situation make themselves known. Intuition is information that is still forming but has not yet coalesced into hard observable facts and figures. It is detected through our other senses, before our mind can organize and analyze it. In some cases our intuition provides us with information that serves as an early warning of what is to come.

Intuition was a primary tool used by the chaos and complexity pioneers. Without a clear understanding of exactly what they were exploring and where it might lead, instincts and intuitions were important guideposts.

Other forms of nonlinear information include storytelling or anecdotal information, myths, and pictures or images.

- Techniques for eliciting nonlinear information include:

  — Recognize that it exists in every situation. You and others in your organization are conduits for this type of information.

  — Include a diverse group in your mapping session. Individuals educated or trained in specific disciplines have intuitions or instincts based on their knowledge and experience.

  — Make sure you identify perking issues and information, and add those to your FutureScape™.

— Draw a picture. In *Beating the Street,* Peter Lynch advises, "Never invest in any idea you can't illustrate with a crayon."[2] Pictures and images stimulate visual thinking. They help us understand what may be difficult to understand with words or quantitative data alone.

For example, a few years ago, while working with the financial division of a large corporation, I discovered a field of smoldering anger and resentment about the company's downsizing and reorganization efforts. The employees were afraid to talk openly about their feelings, so at our next meeting I put paper and crayons on each table. As individuals began arriving for the meeting, I asked each one to draw a picture of what it felt like to be a part of that organization. They hung their pictures on the wall in a space labeled "The Gallery."

We had quite a collection of painful images: people tied to railroad tracks, others swinging from gallows, one standing guard with guns and knives, and another of a car that had run out of gas. The drawing exercise had tapped into a vein of real information.

Acknowledging and working with the emotional content of the images helped to clear the air so that forward movement was possible. And I used the images to brief the executive staff when they joined the meeting later in the day.

The most interesting part of this experience was that the executives themselves were in pain and identified immediately with the images. Over the next few weeks, communication, trust, morale, and productivity improved dramatically.

- Observe and listen to the details of a situation without judgment. Put aside ideas and thoughts based on your previous knowledge of the situation and let the information float.

At first I thought I knew what I was looking for and what I would find. . . . Imagine my surprise when I looked at what I *saw* instead of only seeing what I was looking for.[3]

—Julia Cameron
The Vein of Gold

Principle 7: Perspective is important when viewing chaotic events.

- Distance either reveals or blurs the meaning of movements. Therefore, perspective provides important information about the process of change.

For example, the images of Earth seen from space helped to create a global perspective by blurring individual and national differences. This global "one-world" perspective helped to advance the field of international relations, the environmental movement, joint scientific ventures, and many other global alliances. But because of the distance it could not shed new light on specific local problems such as homelessness or violence. So, it's misleading to guess at meaning until perspective has been considered.

Fractal geometry and the discovery of self-similarity across scales challenges societies, industries, organizations, and individuals to examine their own chaotic episodes with perspective—from afar and in fine detail. The concepts of self-organization and self-similarity have opened exciting new areas of inquiry about the evolution, creativity, and organization of change at its edge.

- When studying a FutureScape™, it's important to see the whole picture, while at the same time recognizing the details and their place and contribution—international, national, regional, or local—to the relationships, connections, and patterns of interaction that are creating changes in your environment.

And finally, remember that not everyone will understand or appreciate the mapping process. And that's okay. Their input will be useful nevertheless. The following comment was made during a mapping session with a large oil and gas exploration company, and the reponse was made by a friend after I told him the story.

> Change is fine, but I'd like some structure to it.
> —Geologist

> Geologists don't see the plum, they see the prune.
> —Photographer
> (*Refers to the fact that geologists study change by looking at millions of years of geological history compressed into a few cubic feet of dirt and rock.*)

How FutureScapes™ Have Been Used to Facilitate Strategic Thinking

FutureScapes™ have been used to facilitate strategic thinking in a variety of situations. Here are some examples.

Strategic Planning: There are three places in the strategic planning process where a FutureScape™ is especially useful. First, creating a FutureScape™ at the beginning of a strategic planning effort will help you identify issues and subjects about which your executive team and/or board need more information prior to its actual planning session. This may include information about business performance, industry trends, competition, changes in customer expectations, new developments, or something out of your normal purview, such as the impact of terrorism on international business travel or the influence of an underground militia on your workforce.

It may also help you recognize a sea change in your environment such as the rapid and dramatic shift to a "managed" health care environment; the growing dominance, through new ownership, of media and entertainment interests in the traditional book publishing industry; or a change in foreign policy and funding priorities following a major international event. By using a FutureScape™ to guide your initial environmental scanning efforts, you are less likely to miss something crucial.

Next, the creation of a FutureScape™ is one of the first steps in an actual planning session. The map serves as the reference point for all the other steps in the planning process and facilitates consensus building on important issues.

And finally, it is important to incorporate the mapping process when reviewing your progress on the plan. Even if it's an abbreviated map, it will serve as a reality check for your progress on existing goals and objectives, and point to the need for possible course corrections. Remember, the map simulates the realities and complexities in the world outside the executive suite.

New Product Development: For product development specialists, the pressure to innovate is enormous. In companies recognized for their success in this area, innovation is an ongoing cycle of idea generation, research, product development, resource allocation, and marketing. And it involves a wide range of professionals, who may not always speak the same language nor have the same priorities.

FutureScapes™ have been used as a vehicle for bringing together these different perspectives early in the process. When used this way a FutureScape™ will help a group identify subtle changes, connections, product gaps, perking developments, and emerging customer needs that point immediately to new ideas and products. It facilitates decision-making and reduces the overall concept-to-customer time frame.

Community Planning: FutureScapes™ have been used to elicit community input into the planning processes of organizations and government agencies with a community mission—local, statewide, or regional. For example, the Colorado Trust, a large heath care foundation, used the mapping process as part of ten focus groups held in different parts of the state. The Trust wanted community input into its program and grant-making priorities. So, the purpose of each of the ten meetings was to ask a cross section of citizens to identify the most important health-related concerns in their community and to see if specific root causes could be identified.

Instead of just listing everyone's favorite projects, the mapping process allowed the participants to see the interrelationships among issues and to identify the most promising leverage points for action. In addition to specific local needs, the mapping process identified *growth* as statewide concern and a significant root cause for many emerging health problems. It also revealed the unique ways in which growth was putting pressure on specific local communities and their existing resources.

Conference Planning: FutureScapes™ have been used to develop conference themes and agendas for a variety of professions, from legal services to banking. By scanning the environment around its target audience, a conference planning committee can easily identify new topics, emerging issues, and innovative approaches that will make their conference a "must attend" on everyone's calendar.

Career Development: A FutureScape™ is a useful tool in helping individuals make career decisions. It helps an individual shift his or her thinking away from the linearity and rigidity of resumé building. It helps them identify new areas of interest and potential by helping them see their history as a portfolio of skills, experiences, and interests that can be reconfigured and redefined in the larger context.

Project Planning: FutureScapes™ have been used successfully in a variety of projects. Scanning the environment of a project helps the project team stay in touch with the larger context and allows them to prioritize and coordinate all of the elements of the project.

For example, lawyers and their legal teams have used FutureScapes™ to develop legal strategy and keep track of the opposing counsel's tactics. Although the judicial system appears orderly, an actual court case is a constantly changing field of play, where surprise maneuvers can shift the direction of a case overnight. The most successful legal teams are those that anticipate where the opposition is going, adapt quickly to new information, and remain flexible in their own strategies.

Curriculum Planning: There are times when a FutureScape™ surfaces disagreements that are so fierce that another tool is needed to move a group forward. I experienced this firsthand while working with a group of parents and educators, who were trying to agree on the basics of a health education curriculum for high school students. In this situation the conflict arose on the topic of sex education. This particular group of parents saw it as their responsibility, not the school's, to provide this information. Whereas the teachers felt that it was their responsibility.

We reached an impasse in the discussion, so I used another tool, a Focused Dialogue Process,[4] to get the conversation moving. The Focused Dialogue Process helped them identify areas of clear agreement, clear disagreement, and areas that needed further discussion. And slowly the group moved toward partial consensus, where in the past there had been only polarization.

In this case, the FutureScape™ helped to surface a perking field of anger and distrust coming from both sides that needed airing. The map helped the group identify the issues to be discussed in the Focused Dialogue Process. It also helped them see the tangle of interrelated issues that kept the conflict in place. But most important, it gave them an opportunity to begin a real conversation, without placing blame.

Training: There are several ways in which to use a FutureScape™ at the beginning of a training session. If a trainer has been hired to present material in a corporate setting, it's usually because the content of the program in some way supports the company's overall strategic directions. In this case, no matter what the topic, it is useful to have the participants create a FutureScape™ of their business environment. This helps them make the connection between the topic and the big picture. It also allows the trainer to use the map as a reference point for highlighting their most important messages.

In other situations, where a trainer has been asked to present to a diverse audience of individual participants, a FutureScape™ can help the trainer focus the material in order to respond to the needs and interests of that particular audience. It also helps a diverse group of individuals make connections with each other.

For example, I am frequently invited by retreat centers, community foundations, or individual organizers to present a workshop or seminar on topics found in this book. In these situations, I always begin with a FutureScape™, but the questions are a little different from those I ask in a corporate setting.

In these settings, the map we are creating is a map for that particular group of people. So, the name of the workshop or seminar goes in the center of the ellipse. I begin by asking each person (if not more than twenty; otherwise I ask participants to call out their answers) what it is about the topic that interests them. Why are they there? What do they hope to get out of the session? And I always conclude by asking them,

"What's perking around this workshop? What could go through this workshop like a bolt of lightning and completely rearrange it for you?" You may also think of a few other questions that would help you understand and connect with a particular group of individuals.

Mapping this type of information will help you understand the environment in which your presentation is being made. It will help you see the connections between and among the participants' interests. It will also give you information about their initial level of knowledge about the topic and serve as a guide for helping you make tight connections between your content and their interests. And finally, it can serve as reference point for closure at the end of your time together.

6

THE NEW PLANNING PARADIGM

What I wish to propose is that complex animals become extinct

not because of a change in their physical adaptation to their

environment, but because of their behavior . . . that behavior

can cease to be responsive to the environment, and lead to

decline and death.

—MICHAEL CRICHTON

The Lost World

"What do we do next?" Executives everywhere are asking this question. "Issues and crises seem to come out of nowhere. I spend most of my time putting out fires. We've tried TQM, reengineering, restructuring, you name it, but nothing seems to work long. Somehow we've lost our focus and the competition is fierce."

The message behind the question is clear: the amount of time and money invested in change efforts yields very little real change, yet change is constant and often unexpected. Everywhere I go, I hear executives of all types wrestling with this paradox. In their efforts to find an answer, I see them grasping at the next idea, theory, or promise. They are stuck on a change treadmill, desperately seeking a miracle.

Most change efforts falter or fail because they are focused on managing an internal change process. Instead of miracles, what we need is a way to see, understand, and respond to the larger external environment in real time, as it is today, not as it was yesterday, last week, or last year. What I'm advocating is a fundamental shift in the way we view change, its relationship to the future, and our ability to influence what is emerging.

The new planning paradigm acknowledges and even embraces the messiness of social, economic, demographic, and political phenomena as well as emerging events and issues. At its heart is strategic thinking based on an in*sight*-fore*sight* model, which recognizes that in a nonlinear world made up of complex adaptive systems, chaos, complexity, and change are the norm. With this new approach to planning, I believe we now have a way to anticipate, respond to, and influence change—before a crisis arises.

Organizations need to see and think about their environment in new ways. Because the issues, challenges, and opportunities any organization will face in the future are perking in its environment today, it's important to find ways to see and organize that information now.

We've grown used to morning headlines filled with surprise events: the Oklahoma City bombing; our federal government, with its sophisticated intelligence network, caught off guard by the bombing of a U.S. military barracks in Saudi Arabia; New York City fighting a dangerous and expensive epidemic of tuberculosis; Microsoft almost missing out on the revolution in cyberspace; and Apple Computer, fighting a losing battle for survival, announces that at last it has buried the hatchet and become Microsoft's partner in creating the technological future.

None of these situations occurred overnight. There must have been clues. The question is "What prevented the principals in each of these situations from seeing and using the information in front of them early in the process?"

The answer, I believe, is that our current strategic planning models are not based on effective strategic thinking. They do not provide a way for us to see and understand the multiple complexities that are creating

WHAT WE KNOW GETS IN THE WAY
OF SEEING WHAT IS . . .

the dynamics of the real world in which our decisions are being made. Nor do they provide a way for us to recognize information that is perking just below the surface. In many cases these perking events are the ones that mushroom overnight and blindside us in the morning.

Most strategic planning models are still too complicated and take too long; they are too confusing, too inflexible, and too disconnected from the dynamics of the real world context they are designed to navigate. And with the primary emphasis on strategy *development*, strategic thinking is often abbreviated or overlooked completely. Without effective strategic thinking, planning is like a shot in the dark. You may be lucky and hit your target, but more likely you'll experience a missed opportunity, a self-wounding ricochet, or a critical blow from an unseen assailant.

Although more democratic than in the past, most planning approaches are still based primarily on quantitative analysis and deterministic forecasting models. Supported by the most sophisticated technology in the world, our ability to analyze, categorize, and colorize quantitative data has diverted our attention. We now have the potential to dazzle ourselves into oblivion, when what we really need is a way to see the big picture context as it really is.

In the new planning paradigm, strategic thinking, the most important step in any planning effort, begins by stepping back and observing the environment as it really is, a complex system of interacting variables. Because the real environment is nonlinear, the strategic thinking must begin as a nonlinear, intuitive process. It must engage the powers of the most sophisticated information processor available today—the human mind.

An emphasis on stakeholder analysis, competitive intelligence, core competencies, and the strengths and weaknesses of an organization have helped to push strategic thinking out past the boardroom walls. But the new science suggests that there is more, much more happening in the environment.

A Brief History of Our Current
Planning Dilemma

Because institutions reflect the cultures in which they evolve, it makes sense that in the early 1900s mechanistic thinking would give birth to scientific management, with its emphasis on understanding the parts of an organization and managing individual tasks. It also makes sense that in recent history the industrialized world just beginning to move forward after World War II and the Korean War would choose to see the future with a strong need for stability and predictability. Change, especially change disguised as chaos, was not something to be embraced.

Forward movement based on this strong need for predictability was reflected in management theories and practice. And like the postwar period in which it began to develop, planning also reflected this desire to minimize the impact of change.

For example, Peter Drucker, widely acknowledged as the father of modern management, met substantial resistance to his view that the postwar world was changing and that organizations needed to find ways to respond and adapt effectively to changes in their external environment. But his 1954 classic, *The Practice of Management*, which laid out the basics of a new approach to planning and managing the work of organizations—management by objectives (MBO)—caught on like a wildfire.

Management by objectives was designed to focus the activities of an organization in ways that ensured forward movement and individual accountability. It promoted the belief that an organization's long-term strategy must be translated into short-term goals and objectives that could be understood and acted on by every manager and employee. In those early days, however, strategy was developed from the inside out with very little attention paid to the external environment.

Organizations used the MBO approach, the precursor to modern strategic planning, successfully for a long time. But as the world began to change more rapidly, many held on to the belief that the future would be simply an extension of the past, and that success would be assured with small incremental adjustments in existing goals and objectives. Many executives endorsed a continuation of what was working without even glancing out the window to see if their world had changed, an approach which soon lost its relevance to the real world.

During the late 1970s and early 1980s, rapid advances in technology and telecommunications created new industries, new markets, and a generation of competitors, both foreign and domestic, that shook the foundations of corporate America. It became painfully clear that the techniques of strategy development needed to be updated in order to relate to a constantly and rapidly changing environment, both locally and globally.

Beginning in the 1980s, enormous resources were spent studying and trying to copy the quality initiatives as well as the planning and management practices of Japanese companies, which had begun to compete with, and in some cases dominate, U.S. and world markets. Those efforts helped to update and shift the planning and management paradigms away from isolated activities toward whole-system processes that are more participatory, flexible, and dynamic.

This approach, now widely accepted, has carried us to the present through a decade of introspection and experimentation. Operational and process-improvement overhauls characterized the early 1990s. Now "growth" is the new corporate mantra. From health care to banking, businesses are looking to capitalize on the strengths of their streamlining efforts.

Following the pain-filled years of corporate downsizing, employment is back up, the economy is strong, small businesses are growing, and despite the public's usual discontent with Washington and the threat of terrorism, there is confidence in our ability to solve our own problems. And even as the ink dries on these words, things are changing.

All of our domestic twists and turns are taking place in a global environment itself being shaped and reshaped by dramatic social, political, and economic changes; by enormous growth in the power and presence of technology; by expanding international markets; and by the ongoing transition to post–Cold War economies. The challenge today is to find a way to see the future in this sea of change.

THINKING ABOUT THE FUTURE

In recent years, efforts to push our thinking and planning toward the future have had many names. But most are adapted from the basic blueprint laid out by three related but somewhat different approaches: preferred futuring, "the vision thing," and scenario building. Organization development practitioners have developed techniques to help groups *create preferred futures.* Visionary leaders *articulate inspirational and challenging images of the future.* While futurists help organizations *anticipate likely future scenarios.*

Preferred futuring answers the question "Who and what do we want to be?" It results in a collective description of a future state toward which the organization moves. A gap exists between the present and the future, and strategies are designed to bridge that gap.

Preferred futuring is supported by information and exercises designed to help groups see, imagine, or envision a desired future state. It often includes descriptions of behavioral outcomes that will help them recognize success: "What will you see, hear, and feel that lets you know you are succeeding?"[1]

Its greatest strength is that it gets groups to think about and commit to a future state that reflects what *they* believe is possible. Its greatest limitation is that it includes an element of wishful thinking.

President Kennedy's 1961 vision of putting "a man on the moon by the end of the decade" has become the modern archetype for inspirational vision statements. This visionary challenge gave America's space program a clear focus and inspired a whole generation, who will never forget Neil Armstrong's confirmation statement on July 20, 1969, "That's one small step for a man, one giant leap for mankind," as he stepped out of Apollo 11's lunar lander and put the first human footprint on the surface of the moon.

Powerful and successful vision statements like this are hard to come by, although that hasn't stopped us from trying. In the last decade, the creation of vision statements has become an industry in itself, as executives and consultants try to craft images of the future that will inspire a company to lift itself out of the doldrums and into a new frontier, where it will be the first to stake a claim.

A clear vision of the future is important, but it needs to be based on a real *foresight process* rather than on one person's inspired image of the future, which too often turns out to be more fantasy than fact. In July 1997, the Eastman Kodak Company shocked analysts and investors by revealing that it had lost more than $100 million so far that year on digital products and services on overall annual sales of $1.5 billion.[2] It had expected to return a profit in 1997 on its annual $500 million investment in this new technology.[3] According to industry experts, CEO George Fisher's vision of Kodak's leadership role in digital photography was either too far ahead of its time, or visionary but misguided, given Kodak's large amateur market.[4] The future may be digital, but it will be a long time before carpooling soccer moms are persuaded to give up their point-and-shoot cameras for something more complicated.

Scenario building, on the other hand, is based on the process of environmental scanning. Environmental scanning is a concept taken from the field of future studies. It is one of a variety of techniques used by futurists to help organizations and policymakers manage issues and make decisions about the future. As used by futurists, environmental scanning involves an analysis of issues, trends, economic forecasts, and other data.

Through this analysis and intuitions about the future, they construct future scenarios or "what ifs" about events and circumstances in the world. Scenarios are given identifying names like, "The Usual," "Jurassic Park Unleashed," or "No. 2 Yahoo!" Scenario-based *planning* results in a number of options or responses to the different scenarios: if this happens, then we go to plan A; but if that happens, then plan B or C is the best move; and if it really gets crazy, then we follow plan ZXX.

Scenario building has been a successful tool in helping organizations think about the future, but it has some limitations. First, it's possible to get so involved in scenario building that you are blinded to unanticipated developments. I actually had someone from the CIA tell me, "We have a scenario for everything that could possibly happen in the world." He told me this the day after the evening news carried pictures of the body of an American soldier being dragged through the streets of Somalia.

With scenario building there is also a gap between the present and the future. The hope is that events occurring in that gap point to one of the scenarios. Scenario building is a little like playing checkers. You have to wait for the other player to make his or her move before you know which of your options will move you safely across the board.

And finally, it takes a while to analyze the data, build the scenarios, and get everyone to agree on the options. Everyone gets focused on the world as you saw it when you started the process, but by the time you reach final agreement on the options, the world has changed, and it's likely that the scenarios are outdated.

Although scenario building is called a foresight technology, it is still primarily a forecasting tool. Based on current data and trends analysis, forecasts are made about the most likely path of events, then scenarios are developed to fit those projections.

Without a doubt, preferred futuring, visioning, and scenario building have moved us forward in our ability to think and plan for the future. All three have helped to shift organizations from reactive to proactive planning, and they all promote consensus building. The question now is "What does the *next generation* look like?" How do we make the final leap from forecasting to foresight?

Visualization is the next revolution in strategic thinking and planning. And the type of visualization that is central to the new planning paradigm is visual thinking—the door to the mind's eye. With the new science, we understand that the future is not information neutral, like a blank canvas awaiting the master's first stroke. Nor is it an ominous wall of darkness moving toward us at warp speed. *The present is the future in its most creative state.*

A recent *BusinessWeek* article entitled "Data Visualization: The Final Frontier?"[5] describes a new multi-media tool developed by Andersen Consulting, which uses various forms of data visualization projected on a wraparound video wall in a futuristic screening room. It's designed to enhance collaborative decision-making.

And a few weeks ago, I received a copy of a news release from Lucent Technologies promoting new data-visualization software developed by

Bell Labs, which is designed to tap the user's intuition and pattern-recognition capabilities by presenting sets of data in graphic form. According to the news release, the system's interactivity is "intended to provide greater insights into business, leading to more informed business decisions . . . and to support the discovery, exploration and analysis of information, patterns and relationships latent within large data-sets."

As we discussed in the chapter on visual thinking, data visualization is just that: *data* visualization. Quantitative data and numerical information are translated into graphic form. Data visualization is a useful tool and an opportunity to develop the skills of visual thinking, but it's not the same as visualizing the multiple complexities that are creating the dynamics of the real world in which your business decisions are being made.

Only the human mind is capable of understanding the multiple complexities in today's world. Both of these examples, however, support the central tenet of the new planning paradigm: *Visual thinking is the key to strategic thinking.*

How a Major Shift in Thinking Takes Place

Although the word "paradigm" is somewhat overused, it is still an important concept in understanding how a change in thinking takes place. A paradigm as described by Thomas Kuhn in his groundbreaking essay, "The Structure of Scientific Revolutions," is an accepted truth, supported by theory and evidence, that for a time provides a story or belief about the way things are.

As we saw in Chapter 1, when Aristotle put forth the belief that the Earth was the center of the universe, with the sun, moon, stars, and other planets revolving around it, theories and models were constructed to support this view. It was adopted by scientific and religious leaders, and for over two thousand years it was the accepted truth or paradigm about the relationship of Earth and man to the rest of the universe.

This paradigm began to shift when Galileo offered proof of the Copernican theory that the Sun, not the Earth, is the center of our planetary system. This shift opened the door for new theories and models, and led Sir Isaac Newton to develop his theory of gravity and to describe the motion of planets in space and time.

In addition to scientific discoveries, events, circumstances, and new technological developments can also create a paradigm shift. And paradigm shifts can occur on any level—personal, organizational, national, or international—as well as within any industry or discipline.

For example, Apollo 11 put a man on the moon and expanded our thinking about the possibilities of manned space flight. "Fast and convenient" is a paradigm that has influenced everything from food to banking. Standards-based education and job skills training have updated the old reading, writing, and arithmetic curricula. And the paradigm shift around smoking is still unfolding, as is the shift from welfare to work.

The introduction of user-friendly computers shifted the paradigm away from large mainframe computers to personalized desktop computing. Competition with Japanese industries shifted the corporate organizational paradigm away from isolated departments and functions to cross-functional thinking and planning. The end of the Cold War has created enormous shifts in foreign policy, military spending, and international and economic alliances. And the shift from manufacturing to services parallels our transition from the industrial age to the post–Cold War knowledge-based information age.

According to Kuhn, a paradigm shifts when evidence or proof of the new is strong enough to pull an "enduring group of adherents" away from the old and toward the new.[6] A paradigm shift is open-ended in that it proposes new questions, redefines old questions, and opens the door for further exploration, discovery, and experimentation.

In this regard, the chaos pioneers were paradigm pioneers. Through their efforts, our view of the world, the process of change, and its relationship to the future have shifted, and with it our need to redefine and shift the way we think about and do planning.

THE NEW PLANNING PARADIGM

The new planning paradigm describes a dynamic, emergent planning process that has three major components: strategic thinking, strategy development, and the allocation of resources, which together result in a clear but flexible and constantly evolving plan of action and implementation. Of these three components, strategic thinking is the most important and the most difficult. It is the process that guides the other two and for which the new science offers the most promise.

*The purpose of strategic thinking in the new planning paradigm is to help an organization **identify, respond to, and influence changes in its environment**.* It is a search for information and options, which will ensure an ongoing competitive advantage for the company given its core skills, strengths, and experience. It involves identifying opportunities for innovation and ways to influence what is emerging, as well as ways to achieve other desired results such as growth, expansion, or the development of new knowledge and expertise. And it is an opportunity to abandon overnight those programs, policies, and strategies that are outdated or ineffective in the present context.

THE NEW PLANNING PARADIGM AS DEFINED
BY THE NEW SCIENCE

From	To
Mechanics of Parts	*Dynamics of the Whole*
Linear	Nonlinear
Static, cause-effect view of individual factors	*Dynamic,* constantly changing field of interactions
Microscopic, local	Wide angle, global
Separateness	Relatedness
Marketplace	Environment
In the old paradigm, it was believed that only by understanding the parts could one make sense of the whole. It also was thought that the world worked like a machine with clock-work precision	In the new paradigm, the parts of a system can be understood only in relationship to the dynamics of the whole. The whole is a constantly changing field of connections, relationships, and patterns of interaction
Component thinking	Seeing and thinking in wholes
Time cards, task analysis	Complex adaptive systems
Problem solving	Butterfly Effect, system feedback
Brainstorming	Self-organization, adaptation
Polarization	Environmental scanning plus mapping
Structure	*Process*
Structure creates process	Underlying processes and interactions of a system's variables create self-organizing patterns, shapes, and structures

Focuses on organizational pathology	Focuses on organizational potential
Organizational chart as truth and indicator of entitlements, bureaucracy, and hierarchy	Organizational chart as a guide to centers of core activity, sources of energy, and innovation
Pays attention to policies and procedures that are usually fixed and inflexible	Pays attention to initial conditions, perking information, emerging events, and strange attractors
Standing committees	Ad hoc working groups, networks
Politics	Learning

Planning As an Event	*Strategic Thinking and Planning as Ongoing Processes*
Annual event, often with data as the centerpiece	Strategic thinking is the center-piece and is everyone's ongoing responsibility
Plan developed by strategic planning staff, committee, or consultants	Whole-system input into planning process
Board approves committee recommendations or consultant's report	Plan of action and implementation are flexible and constantly evolving in response to emerging conditions

The Future Is Tomorrow	*The Future Is Happening Today*
Scenario building, preferred futuring, future "search" efforts	Identify and influence perking data, initial conditions
Leaders who rely on formula and reputation	Leaders who understand the context and respond effectively
Consensus decision-making	Decisive leadership plus appropriate consensus building

Forecasting Through Data Analysis	*Foresight Through Visual Synthesis*
Quantitative data and questions drive the planning process	Assumptions, critical planning issues, and questions are checked/answered in the big picture context
Data visualization	Visual thinking, which helps us synthesize qualitative information and quantitative data
Intellectual understanding	Intuitive knowing plus intellectual understanding
Left hemisphere skills only	Engages the whole brain

Controlling, Stabilizing, or Managing Change	*Responding to and Influencing Change As It Is Emerging*
Dinosaur behavior	Entrepreneurial behavior
Sees change as a threat	Sees change as an opportunity
Leads to stagnation and extinction	Leads to renewal and growth
Anxiety, fear, confusion, finger-pointing, and self-preservation behaviors are pervasive	A spirit of exploration, learning, openness to change, pride, and mutual support are pervasive
	Looks for perking data, initial conditions, and strange attractors
	Knows how to create and use a strategic intelligence network for both qualitative and quantitative information
Shareholder value is primary	Responding to and influencing changes in the environment are primary

Recognizes only capital-based assets	Portfolio of skills and experience that can be redefined and reconfigured
Slow to develop new products and client services	Understands how to use emerging conditions for innovation and to develop new products and services
Leadership is responsible for success	Everyone is responsible for success

IN WHAT WAYS IS THIS APPROACH TO PLANNING MORE EFFECTIVE?

Planning models are either horizontal, vertical, or sometimes even circular, but the basic elements are the same: a vision and mission statement, goals, and objectives. The difference in the new planning paradigm is that strategic thinking, facilitated by the use of a FutureScape™, is the centerpiece. Using this model, all the other steps in the planning process are connected to the realities and the multiple complexities of the big picture context in which your decisions are being made.

The FutureScape™ allows you to see the future as it is emerging. It is in a sense an organic model out of which strategy emerges. Your future challenges are obvious and the leverage points become clear. And every step of the planning process is defined and then redefined in terms of a constantly changing environment.

For example, a medical practice looks out its window and sees an aging but health conscious baby-boom population and expands its thinking from "taking care of sick people" to "keeping our community healthy." The Xerox Corporation, recognizing enormous competition in the copy-related products market, sees integrated networks and digital technology on the horizon, and redefines itself as "the document company" in a changing technological environment.[7] By shifting its focus from copiers to documents, Xerox expanded its options by positioning itself as the leader in helping organizations make the transition from stand-alone single-purpose copy machines to "networked document creation systems."[8] The new systems reduce document handling time by allowing documents to be scanned-in or created at a single workstation, transmitted to multiple locations or around the world, and modified before the first paper copy is ever printed.[9]

And a nonprofit organization that has for years provided housing and employment opportunities for people with disabilities suddenly finds itself in a managed care environment in a state with an enormous influx of healthy elderly. It decides to use its expertise to expand into the construction and management of retirement living centers, with the expectation that this new source of revenue will strengthen its ability to continue providing services to its primary population.

In this model, strategic thinking facilitated by a FutureScape™ fills in the gaps left by preferred futuring, inspired visioning, and scenario building. The way in which you define your business, its long-term aspirations, and your immediate and longer-term options arise out of the present context and emerging phenomena. The key to success is to understand and use the basics of strategic thinking as defined by the new science.

STRATEGIC THINKING AND THE NEW SCIENCE

I. **Understand the context.** The context is global. You must consider all aspects of the global environment—local, regional, national, and international.

II. **Understand the *dynamics* of change in the global context as described by the new science.** In complex adaptive systems, change occurs through the process of adaptation set in motion through the Butterfly Effect. Through this process a new self-organizing pattern, shape, or structure emerges.

III. **Use the Seven Principles of Strategic Thinking as Defined by the New Science.**

  1. Look at whole systems, not just their parts.
  2. There is a relationship between order and disorder, and self-organizing change occurs as a result of their interactions.
  3. A small event in one sector can cause tremendous turbulence in another.
  4. Maps, models, and visual images make it easier to see connections, relationships, and patterns of interaction.
  5. Scanning across disciplines and industries is the key to seeing emerging conditions, paradigm shifts, and opportunities for innovation.
  6. Nonlinear thinking is critical to recognizing clues about changes in the environment.
  7. Perspective is important when viewing chaotic events.

IV. **Remember that strategic thinking has two major components, which are facilitated by the use of a FutureScape™ and the process of visual thinking.**

Insight About the Present	_Foresight About the Future_
Prior to a strategic planning session and the creation of a FutureScape™:	Know what you're looking for in the FutureScape™:
• _Prepare yourself._ Insight comes after intense preparation or study of the problem to which it responds.	• Movement of the whole, emerging conditions, and your system's new initial conditions.

- Connections, relationships, and patterns of interaction.

—Know your history.

—Inaccessible or invisible phenomena and relationships.

—Know your business.

—Know your industry.

—Find out what everyone else in your organization knows about what's happening in these key areas.

—An understanding of abstract concepts.

—Know the assumptions on which your business operates.

—Validation of data and assumptions or the identification of areas where you need more information.

—Read outside your field. Be curious about many unrelated subjects.

—A new synthesis of information and relationships among disciplines.

And remember:

- The key to *insight* is seeing the underlying connections and interactions that might otherwise be missed.

- The key to *foresight* is identifying your system's new *initial conditions* as well as the self-organizing connections, relationships, and patterns of interaction in the larger context.

- The key to *influencing the future* is to apply your thinking and planning resources NOW to emerging conditions, issues, and opportunities.

Understanding and using the new science as the basis for strategic thinking will help you focus your resources in ways that will allow you to influence the future—today!

N O T E S

INTRODUCTION

1. Wetherell (May 5, 1996).
2. Herring (1996), p. 50.
3. Salter (1995), p. 3.
4. Ibid., p. 4.
5. Ibid., p. 5.
6. Ibid., p. 5–10.

CHAPTER ONE: LISTEN TO THE FOOTPRINTS

Special note to the reader: In the first part of Chapter 1, the history of science through the medieval period, I relied heavily on *The Beginnings of Western Science* by David C. Lindberg, professor of the history of science and director of the Institute for Research on the Humanities at the University of Wisconsin. I lived with this book for weeks and it became a friend as well as an invaluable and highly readable resource for this chapter.

One of the points the author makes throughout the book is the importance of setting aside our tendency to judge history and to look at it instead for what it tells us about those whose thinking it reflects. This sense of openness is what makes this book so interesting. Without the intrusion of critique, it is easy to follow the development of scientific thinking across many generations and cultures.

In a telephone conversation, Dr. Lindberg referred me to two books, which became my primary references for the section on the Scientific Revolution. *The Construction of Modern Science* by Richard S. Westfall is a detailed and straightforward account of the scientific developments during this period of history. *The Scientific Revolution* by Steven Shapin weaves together stories about the key scientific achievements and the cultural context in which they developed.

I owe a great deal of thanks to these three authors, whose books, when used together, create a fascinating and informative account of the history of science through the seventeenth century. And I apologize to them for the many abridgments and omissions I made in the subjects they covered so thoroughly.

1. LaViolette (1995).
2. Hughes (February 13, 1995).
3. Campbell (1990); Bonnefoy (1991).
4. Lindberg (1992), p. 11; see special note, p. 155).
5. Boorstin (1994), p. 35.
6. McBrien (1995); Strayer (1989).
7. Bachrach (1995); Hroch and Skybová (1988).
8. Boorstin (1983), p. 141.
9. Westfall (1971), p. 38.
10. Shapin (1996), p. 36.
11. Hawking (1988), p. 64.
12. Stewart (1995), p. 2, 14.

CHAPTER TWO: BUTTERFLIES AND HURRICANES

1. Gleick (1987), p. 11–31. The references to Edward Lorenz are adapted from Gleick's description of these same events. His book is the best introduction to the people, their work, and the discoveries that brought chaos theory into focus. I highly recommend it.
2. Stewart (1995).
3. Mandelbrot (1983), p. 1.
4. Hawking (1987), p. 53.
5. Stewart (1995), p. 113–15; Capra (1996), p. 126–28.
6. Stewart (1995), p. 58–59.
7. Hawking (1987), p. 29–33.
8. Hawking (1987).
9. Kauffman (1995); Capra (1996).
10. Kauffman (1996), p. 27.

CHAPTER THREE: GETTING STARTED:
REAL WORLD APPLICATIONS

1. Roberts et al., February 24, 1994.
2. Grove (1996), p. 32.
3. Ibid., p. 62.
4. Gerstner, p. 5.
5. Motorola (1994).

CHAPTER FOUR: VISUAL THINKING

1. Ohmae (1982), p. 4.
2. Grandin (1995), p. 20–21.
3. Hooper (1986); Siler (1990); West (1991).
4. *Scientific American,* September 1992; *Scientific American,* Special Issue 1997.
5. Newmarch (1905), p. 274–75.
6. May (1975); Harman (1984); Hadamard (1945).
7. Penrose (1989), p. 418–19.
8. Abell (1994), p. 5–6.
9. Tesla (1982), p. 33.
10. Pickover (1994) in Pickover and Tewksbury, p. 2.
11. Freidhoff (1989), p. 16.
12. Colona (1994), p. 184–85.
13. Ibid., p. 185–91.
14. Gleick (1987), p. 38–39.
15. Ibid., p. 30–31.
16. Mandlebrot (1983), p. 1.
17. Siler (1996), p. 8.

CHAPTER FIVE: FROM FORECASTING TO FORESIGHT

1. Ohmae (1982), p. 13.
2. Lynch (1993), p. 27
3. Cameron (1996), p. 115–16.
4. The Focused Dialogue Process is a consensus-building model I developed while working with the U.S. Senate.
5. Wycoff (1991).

SPECIAL NOTE TO THE READER: **A FutureScape™ is NOT a mindmap.** Mindmapping®, a technique developed by Tony Buzan in the 1970s, helps *you organize information visually* on a specific subject.[5] A FutureScape™, on the other hand, helps *you see the self-organizing behavior* of the big-picture context in which your decisions are being made.

There are obvious similarities, in that both techniques engage the capacities of the whole brain by using visual techniques, but there are also some important differences in terms of principles, methods, and applications. In a sense they are cousins, and those of you who have used mindmapping will feel at home with the process of creating a FutureScape™ .

Mindmap®

The process of *mind*mapping is used to create a visual outline for a meeting or document, or as a nonlinear alternative to traditional lists, outlines, brainstorming, or note taking. Helps you organize your thinking, thus the name.

You organize the information by clustering or some other method as the map is being created.

A mindmap is an idea or subject diagram and looks similar to the type of sentence diagram many of us learned to make in school.

Uses words and images to help you organize *content*—ideas, thoughts, and next steps. Creates a sense of understanding, clarity, and organization.

A powerful tool for helping you focus. May be a useful tool in the planning process following the use of a Future-Scape™.

FutureScape™

The process of creating a Future-Scape™ results in a visual representation of the larger environment of the system or issue question being considered. Helps you see the big picture and the changes that are beginning to shape the future, thus the name.

You do not try to organize the information while you are creating the map.

Simulates a live-action weather map. Helps you recognize the multiple complexities—connections, relationships, and patterns of interaction—that are creating the real world environment in which your decisions are being made.

Uses words and images to help you understand the self-organizing dynamics of the big-picture *context*. Requires a willingness to tolerate ambiguity, uncertainty, and messiness long enough for the map to engage both your intuition and intellect. The map will speak to your deeper levels of awareness if you have the patience to listen.

The first step in strategic thinking. Allows you to develop *insight* about the present and *foresight* about the future.

CHAPTER SIX: THE NEW PLANNING PARADIGM

1. Jacobs (1994), p. 102.
2. Nelson and White, p. 6.
3. Ibid.
4. Ibid.
5. Coy, p. 150.
6. Kuhn (1970), p. 10.
7. Chakravarty, June 6, 1994.
8. Weinberg, June 6, 1994.
9. Chakravarty, June 6, 1994.

GLOSSARY

ATTRACTOR: The end state toward which a dynamical system moves. For example, if you throw a handful of marbles into a bowl, they will eventually all come to rest at the bottom. The bottom of the bowl is the attractor, a specific point. In other cases, the attractor is a cycle, like the back and forth movement of the pendulum in a grandfather clock. And then there are systems that never settle into a steady state and those are said to have strange attractors. See *strange attractor.*

BUTTERFLY EFFECT: A metaphorical term describing the image of a butterfly fluttering its wings in Asia and causing a hurricane in the Atlantic. The Butterfly Effect describes the way small systems interact with large systems through a *sensitive dependence on initial conditions;* this means that points of instability or vulnerability to new influences exist everywhere in a complex nonlinear system. Small changes have a multiplier effect on future events. Small differences multiply upward, expanding into larger and larger systems, changing conditions all along the way, eventually causing unexpected consequences at a broader level sometime in the future.

CHAOS THEORY: The popular name for dynamical systems theory or nonlinear studies. Chaos theory says that the behavior of a dynamical system is highly nonlinear, meaning that it is difficult to predict its outcome or future state, because the variables are interacting constantly with each other. A nonlinear system is not modular; it cannot be taken apart and added back together again. The weather is a good example of a nonlinear system. Chaos theory developed as scientists began to see and understand the dynamics at work behind the seemingly random behavior of nonlinear systems. Through their research and the use of powerful computer graphics, scientists have demonstrated that beneath the seemingly chaotic behavior of a nonlinear system, there is order—a type of self-organizing pattern, shape, or structure.

COMPLEXITY OR COMPLEXITY THEORY: Describes the way a complex *adaptive* system responds to new information to which it is sensitive through the process of adaptation.

COMPLEX ADAPTIVE SYSTEMS: Nonlinear systems that have the ability to process and incorporate new information. Most of the world is made up of complex adaptive systems. The social world—the world of people, politics, and commerce—is one vast complex adaptive system with many interconnecting points. Complex adaptive systems change or respond to new information to which they are sensitive through a process of *adaptation*.

ENVIRONMENTAL SCANNING: An ongoing effort to gather information about changes in an individual's or organization's environment. It provides a big-picture context for decision-making. *Environmental scanning is where strategic thinking begins.* Because the issues and challenges any organization will face in the future are perking in its environment today, it's important to find ways to see and organize that information now.

FRACTAL GEOMETRY: A new concept in geometry, which incorporates the complex, irregular, and changeable qualities of a structure, like the jaggedness of a shoreline or the roughness in a steel beam. Classical Euclidean geometry used simple concepts like cones, spheres, and lines to represent the shapes and forms of nature and man-made structures.

FRACTALS OR FRACTAL IMAGES: Through the use of powerful computer graphics it is now possible to create detailed pictures of the behavior or movement of a nonlinear system over time. These pictures capture the delicate patterns as they are emerging within the behavior of a nonlinear system. Also used to describe photographs that show repeated or self-similar patterns in the natural world. An example would be a single fern plant, where every branch is similar to its others, and a natural fern garden in the forest, where the patterns are repeated over and over.

FUTURESCAPE™: An artistic representation of an organization's environment. It includes issues, challenges, opportunities, and other factors affecting or influencing the organization. The map or picture allows an individual or a group to synthesize an enormous amount of data immediately by capturing the information visually. A FutureScape™ simulates a live-action weather map.

LORENZ ATTRACTOR: The first graphic image of a *strange* attractor. Named after Edward Lorenz, a research meteorologist and mathematician, working in the 1960s at the Massachusetts Institute of Technology. Lorenz studied the dynamics of convection, then translated the behavior of those systems into a set of numbers. By projecting the behavior of this set of numbers over time, he generated the first images of *chaos*, or the order hidden within the seemingly chaotic behavior of a nonlinear system.

NONLINEAR: Not linear or modular. The pieces cannot be taken apart and added back together the same way. For example, the path of a wildfire is nonlinear. It depends on many things—moisture on the ground and in the trees, wind and weather conditions, the lay of the land, the types of trees, and the fire-fighting interventions of people. These conditions are changing constantly, making it impossible to predict the fire's path.

STRANGE ATTRACTOR: The collection of variables that holds a chaotic nonlinear system together and gives it its shape. The attraction of the variables creates the edges or boundaries of the pattern and the interactions of the variables create the internal design that never repeats itself. Think about a photograph of a hurricane. The familiar spiral shape or pattern is created by the attraction and active relationship of the elements making up the hurricane system.

STRATEGIC THINKING: The obvious precursor to any strategy development or planning session. It begins with *exploration* of the environment, an intuitive, visual, creative process that results in a synthesis of emerging themes, issues, patterns, connections, and opportunities. It has two major components: insight about the present and foresight about the future.

B I B L I O G R A P H Y

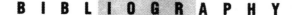

A World Transformed: Our Reflections on Ending the Cold War. 1996. KUHT, Houston Public Television.

Abell, Arthur M. 1994. *Talks with Great Composers.* New York: Citadel Press.

Allen, Pat B. 1995. *Art Is a Way of Knowing.* London: Shambala.

Anton, Ted, and Rick McCourt (eds.). 1995. *The New Science Journalists.* New York: Ballantine Books.

Arnheim, Rudolf. 1969. *Visual Thinking.* Berkeley: University of California Press.

Associated Press. 1996. "Flashover took area power out." *Rocky Mountain News.* July 21, 1996, p. 24A.

Augros, Robert, and George Stanciu. 1988. *The New Biology.* Boston: Shambala.

Bachrach, Deborah. 1995. *Inquisition.* San Diego: Lucent Books.

Baraka. 1993. A film by Ron Fricke and Mark Magidson. A Mark Magidson Production.

Barker, Joel Arthur. 1992. *Future Edge.* New York: William Morrow.

Bateson, Gregory. 1979. *Mind and Nature: A Necessary Unity.* New York: Bantam Books.

Beckhard, Richard, and Reuban T. Harris. 1987. *Organizational Transitions.* Reading, MA: Addison-Wesley.

Berry, Michael V., I. C. Percival, and N. O. Weiss. 1987. *Dynamical Chaos: Proceedings of a Royal Society Discussion Meeting Held on 4 and 5 February 1987.* Princeton: Princeton University Press.

Berger, John. *Ways of Seeing.* 1972. London: British Broadcasting Corporation and Penguin Books.

Bezold, Clement (ed.). 1978. *Anticipatory Democracy: People in the Politics of the Future.* New York: Random House.

Blakney, R. B. (trans.). 1955. *The Way of Life by Lao Tzu.* New York: Mentor.

Bloomer, Carolyn M. (ed., second edition). 1990. *Principles of Visual Perception.* New York: Design Press.

Bohm, David. 1980. *Wholeness and the Implicate Order.* New York: ARK Paperbacks.

Bohm, David, and Mark Edwards. 1991. *Changing Consciousness*. New York: Harper-SanFrancisco.

Bonnefoy, Yves (comp.), and Wendy Doniger (trans.). 1991. *Greek and Egyptian Mythologies*. Chicago: University of Chicago Press.

Boorstin, Daniel J. 1983. *The Discoverers*. New York: Vintage Books.

———. 1992. *The Creators*. New York: Vintage Books.

———. 1994. *Cleopatra's Nose*. New York: Vintage Books.

Brandenburger, Adam M., and Barry J. Nalebuff. "Inside Intel." *Harvard Business Review*. November–December 1996, p. 168–75.

Bridges, William. 1980. *Transitions: Making Sense of Life's Changes*. Reading, MA: Addison-Wesley.

Briggs, John. 1992. *Fractals: The Patterns of Chaos*. New York: Touchstone.

Brockman, John, and Katinka Matson (eds.). 1995. *How Things Are*. New York: William Morrow.

Browne, Malcolm W. "New Vistas Open for Earthbound Astronomers." *New York Times*. February 11, 1997, p. C-1.

———. "Math Gets Friendly, With Fewer Numbers and a Flair for Fun." *New York Times*. February 21, 1997, p. B-19.

Bryne, John A. "Strategic Planning." *BusinessWeek*. August 26, 1996, p. 46–53.

Bunker, Ted. "Physicist Richard P. Feynman: In Pursuit of Knowledge, He Took Nothing for Granted." *Investor's Business Daily*. March 24, 1995.

Cameron, Julia. 1996. *The Vein of Gold*. New York: G.P. Putnam's Sons.

Campbell, Joseph. 1990. *Transformations of Myth Through Time*. New York: Harper & Row.

Capra, Fritjof. 1975. *The Tao of Physics*. Boston: Shambala Publications.

———. 1991. *Belonging to the Universe*. HarperSanFrancisco.

———. 1996. *The Web of Life*. New York: Anchor Books.

Casti, John. "Confronting Science's Logical Limits." *Scientific American*. October 1996, p. 102–5.

———. 1994. *COMPLEXification: Explaining A Paradoxical World Through the Science of Surprise*. New York: HarperPerennial.

Chakravarty, Subrata N. "Back in Focus." *Forbes*. June 6, 1994, p. 72–74.

Chalmers, David J. "The Puzzle of Conscious Experience." *Scientific American*. December 1995. p. 80–86.

Chorafas, Dimitris N. 1994. *Chaos Theory in Financial Markets*. Chicago: Probus Publishing.

Clark, Ronald W. 1971. *Einstein: The Life and Times*. New York: The World Publishing.

Coates, Joseph F., and Staff. 1986. *Issues Management*. Mt. Airy, MD: Lomond Publications.

Cohen, Jack, and Ian Stewart. 1994. *The Collapse of Chaos*. New York: Penguin Books.

Colonna, Jean-Francois. 1994. "Scientific Display: A Means of Reconciling Artists and Scientists," in Clifford A. Pickover and Stuart K. Tewksbury (eds.). *Frontiers of Scientific Visualization*. New York: John Wiley & Sons.

Combs, Allan, and Mark Holland. 1990. *Synchronicity: Science, Myth and the Trickster*. New York: Paragon House.

Corcoran, Elizabeth. "Ordering Chaos." *Scientific American*. August 1991, p. 96–98.

Cornwell, John (ed.). 1995. *Nature's Imagination*. New York: Oxford University Press.

Coveney, Peter, and Roger Highfield. 1995. *Frontiers of Complexity: The Search for Order in a Chaotic World*. New York: Fawcett Columbine.

Coy, Peter. "Data Visualization: The Final Frontier?" *BusinessWeek*. October 28, 1996, p. 150.

Crichton, Michael. 1995. *The Lost World*. New York: Alfred A. Knopf.

Crosby, Alfred W. 1997. *The Measure of Reality: Quantification and Western Society, 1250–1600*. New York: Cambridge University Press.

Csikszentmihalyi, Mihaly. 1996. *Creativity: Flow and the Psychology of Discovery and Invention*. New York: HarperCollins.

Cvitanovic, Predrag (ed.). 1989. *Universality in Chaos (second ed)*. Philadelphia: Institute of Physics Publishing.

Davies, Paul. 1995. *About Time: Einstein's Unfinished Revolution*. New York: Touchstone.

Davis, Kenneth C. 1992. *Don't Know Much About Geography*. New York: Avon Books.

Davis, Stanley M. 1987. *Future Perfect*. Reading, MA: Addison-Wesley.

Davis, Stan, and Bill Davidson. 1991. *2020 Vision*. New York: Simon & Schuster.

de Bono, Edward. 1992. *Serious Creativity*. New York: HarperBusiness.

Drake, Stillman. 1978. *Galileo at Work: His Scientific Biography*. Chicago: University of Chicago Press.

Drucker, Peter. 1954. *The Practice of Management*. New York: Harper & Row.

———. 1985. *Innovation and Entrepreneurship*. New York: HarperBusiness

———. 1989. *The New Realities*. New York: Harper & Row.

———. 1993. *Post-Capitalist Society*. New York: HarperBusiness.

———. 1995. *Managing in a Time of Great Change*. New York: Truman Tally Books/ Dutton.

Edwards, Betty. 1989. *Drawing on the Right Side of the Brain (revised ed.)*. Los Angeles: Jeremy P. Tarcher.

Ehrenhalt, Alan. "Keepers of the Dismal Faith." *New York Times*. February 23, 1997, p. E-13.

Eisley, Loren. 1978. *The Star Thrower*. San Diego: A Harvest/HBJ Book.

Feibleman, James K. 1984. *Understanding Oriental Philosophy (revised ed.)*. New York: Meridian.

Ferguson, Marilyn. 1980. *The Aquarian Conspiracy*. Los Angeles: J.P. Tarcher.

Feynman, Richard P. 1967. *The Character of Physical Law.* Cambridge: MIT Press.

———. 1985. *Surely You're Joking, Mr. Feynman.* New York: Bantam Books.

———. 1995. *Six Easy Pieces.* Reading, MA: Helix Books and Addison-Wesley.

Finke, Ronals A., Thomas B. Ward, and Steven M. Smith. 1992. *Creative Cognition.* Cambridge, MA: A Bradford Book, The MIT Press.

Fox, Matthew, and Rupert Sheldrake. 1996. *The Physics of Angels: Exploring the Realm Where Science and Spirit Meet.* New York: HarperSanFrancisco.

Freedman, David H. 1994. *Brainmakers.* New York: Simon & Schuster.

Freiberg, Kevin, and Jackie Freiberg. 1996. *NUTS! Southwest Airlines's Crazy Recipe for Business and Personal Success.* Austin, TX: Bard Press.

Friedhoff, Richard Mark. 1989. *Visualization: The Second Computer Revolution.* New York: Harry N. Abrams.

Fuller, R. Buckminster. 1981. *Critical Path.* New York: St. Martin's Press.

Gardner, Howard. 1995. *Leading Minds: An Anatomy of Leadership.* New York: BasicBooks.

Gelernter, David. 1994. *The Muse in the Machine.* New York: The Free Press.

Gerstner, Lou. *ThinkTwice.* An IBM Employee Publication, special edition. December 1993. p. 5.

Glanz, James. "Debating the Big Questions." *Science.* August 30, 1996, p. 1168.

Gleick, James. 1987. *Chaos: Making A New Science.* New York: Penguin Books.

———. 1992. *Genius.* New York: Pantheon Books.

Gorbachev, Mikhail. 1987. *Perestroika: New Thinking for Our Country and the World.* New York: Harper & Row.

Gore, Vice President Al. 1993. *Earth in the Balance.* New York: Plume.

Gorman, James. "Consciousness Studies: From Stream to Flood." *New York Times.* April 29, 1997, p. B 7–9.

Grandin, Temple. 1995. *Thinking in Pictures.* New York: Doubleday.

Grove, Andrew S. 1996. *Only the Paranoid Survive.* New York: Doubleday.

Hadamard, Jacques. 1945. *The Psychology of Invention in the Mathematical Field.* New York: Dover Publications.

Haley, Jay. 1986. *Uncommon Therapy.* New York: W.W. Norton.

Hall, Edward T. 1981. *Beyond Culture.* New York: Anchor Press

Hall, Nina (ed.). 1991. *Exploring Chaos: A Guide to the New Science of Disorder.* New York: W.W. Norton.

Hall, Stephen S. 1992. *Mapping the Next Millennium: The Discovery of New Geographies.* New York: Random House.

Hamel, Gary. "Strategy as Revolution." *Harvard Business Review.* July–August 1996, p. 69–82.

Hamel, Gary, and C. K. Prahalad. "Strategic Intent." *Harvard Business Review.* May–June 1989, p. 63–76.

———. 1994. *Competing for the Future.* Boston: Harvard Business School Press.

Handy, Charles. 1994. *The Age of Paradox.* Boston: Harvard Business School Press.

Hargittai, Istvan, and Magdolna Hargittai. 1994. *Symmetry: A Unifying Concept.* Bolinas, CA: Shelter Publications.

Harman, Willis. 1988. *Global Mind Change.* Indianapolis, IN: Knowledge Systems.

Harman, Willis, and John Horman. 1990. *Creative Work.* Indianapolis, IN: Knowledge Systems.

Harman, Willis, and Howard Rheingold. 1984. *Higher Creativity.* New York: G.P. Putnam's Sons.

Hawking, Stephen W. 1987. *A Brief History of Time.* New York: Bantam Books.

Hillman, James. 1996. *The Soul's Code.* New York: Random House.

Herring, Thomas A. "The Global Positioning System." *Scientific American.* February 1996, p. 44–50.

Hofstadter, Douglas R. 1985. *Metamagical Themas: Questing for the Essence of Mind and Pattern.* New York: Bantam Books.

Holland, John H. 1995. *Hidden Order: How Adaptation Builds Complexity.* Reading, MA: Helix Books.

Hooper, Judith, and Dick Teresi. 1986. *The 3-Pound Universe.* New York: G.P. Putnam's Sons.

Hroch, Miroslav, and Anna Skybová. 1988. *Ecclesia Militans: The Inquisition.* New York: Dorset Press.

Hughes, Robert. "Behold the Stone Age." *Time Magazine.* February 13, 1995, p. 52–62.

Hunt, Morton. 1993. *The Story of Psychology.* New York: Doubleday.

Jacobs, Robert W. 1991. *Cathedral Building: Integrating Strategy Development, Large Systems Change, and Real-Time Implementation.* Unpublished thesis. School of Business and Management (Organization Development), Pepperdine University.

———. 1994. *Real Time Strategic Change.* San Francisco: Berrett-Koehler Publishers.

Jamison, Kay Redfield. "Manic-Depressive Illness and Creativity." *Scientific American.* February 1995, p. 62–67.

Johnson, George. 1996. *Fire in the Mind.* New York: Alfred A. Knopf.

Kane, Gordon. 1995. *The Particle Garden: Our Universe as Understood by Particle Physicists.* Reading, MA: Helix Books.

Kanter, Rosabeth Moss. 1983. *The Change Masters.* New York: Touchstone.

———. 1989. *When Giants Learn to Dance.* New York: Simon & Schuster.

———. 1995. *World Class.* New York: Simon & Schuster.

Kaptchuk, Ted. 1983. *The Web That Has No Weaver.* New York: Congdron & Weed.

Katzenbach, Jon R., and the RCL Team. 1995. *Real Change Leaders.* New York: Times Business.

Kauffman, Stuart. "Antichaos and Adaptation." *Scientific American.* August 1991, p. 78.

———. 1995. *At Home in the Universe.* New York: Oxford University Press.

Kellert, Stephen H. *In the Wake of Chaos.* Chicago: University of Chicago Press.

Kidder, Rushworth M. 1989. *Reinventing the Future.* Cambridge, MA: MIT Press.

Koestenbaum, Peter. 1987. *The Heart of Business.* San Francisco: Saybrook Publishing.

Krauss, Lawrence M. 1989. *The Fifth Essence: The Search for Dark Matter in the Universe.* New York: Basic Books.

Kuhn, Thomas. 1970. *The Structure of Scientific Revolutions (second ed.).* Chicago: University of Chicago Press.

Laqueur, Walter. 1989. *The Long Road to Freedom: Russia and Glasnost.* New York: Charles Scribner's Sons.

LaViolette, Paul. 1995. *Beyond the Big Bang.* Rochester, VT: Park Street Press.

Lee, Chris. "The Vision Thing." *Training.* February 1993, p. 25–34.

Leland, Nita. 1990. *The Creative Artist.* Cincinnati: North Light Books.

Levitt, Theodore. 1986. *The Marketing Imagination.* New York: The Free Press.

Lewin, Roger. 1992. *Complexity.* New York: Macmillan Publishing.

Lindberg, David C. 1992. *The Beginnings of Western Science.* Chicago: University of Chicago Press.

Lorenz, Edward N. "Deterministic Nonperiodic Flow." *Journal of the Atmospheric Sciences.* March 1963, p. 130–41.

———. 1993. *The Essence of Chaos.* Seattle: University of Washington Press.

Lynch, Peter, with John Rothchild. 1993. *Beating the Street.* New York: Simon & Schuster.

Mainzer, Klaus. 1994. *Thinking in Complexity: The Complex Dynamics of Matter, Mind, and Mankind.* New York: Springer-Verlag.

Makridakis, Spyros, and Steven C. Wheelwright. 1989. *Forecasting Methods for Management.* New York: John Wiley & Sons.

Mallery, Garrick. 1972. *Picture-Writing and the American Indians. Vol. Two.* New York: Dover Publications.

Mandelbrot, Benoit B. 1983. *The Fractal Geometry of Nature.* New York: W.H. Freeman.

May, Rollo. 1975. *The Courage to Create.* New York: W.W. Norton.

McBrien, Richard P. (gen. ed.). 1995. *The HarperCollins Encyclopedia of Catholicism.* New York: HarperCollins.

McDaniel, Melissa. 1994. *Stephen Hawking: Revolutionary Physicist.* New York: Chelsea House Publications.

McGaine, Michael. 1991. *An Eye for Fractals.* Redwood City: Addison-Wesley.

McGlashan, Alan. 1988. *The Savage and Beautiful Country.* Einsiedeln, Switzerland: Daimon Verlag.

McNeill, William H. 1976. *Plagues and Peoples.* New York: Anchor Books.

Micklethwait, John, and Adrian Wooldridge. 1996. *The Witch Doctors.* New York: Times Books.

Miller, Arthur I. 1996. *Insights of Genius: Imagery and Creativity in Science and Art.* New York: Copernicus.

Miller, James Grier. 1978. *Living Systems*. New York: McGraw-Hill.

Mintzberg, Henry. 1989. *Mintzberg on Management*. New York: The Free Press.

————. 1994. *The Rise and Fall of Strategic Planning*. New York: The Free Press.

————. "Musings on Management." *Harvard Business Review*. July–August 1996, p. 61–67.

Mitroff, Ian I. 1987. *Business NOT as Usual*. San Francisco: Jossey-Bass Publishers.

Monmonier, Mark. 1995. *Drawing the Lines: Tales of Maps and Cartocontroversy*. New York: Henry Holt.

Morgan, Gareth. 1988. *Riding the Waves of Change*. San Francisco: Jossey-Bass Publishers.

Morowitz, Harold. "Why Complexity Theory?" *Complexity*. 1995/1996. New York: John Wiley & Sons.

Morris, Richard. 1990. *The Edges of Science*. New York: Prentice Hall Press.

Motorola Museum of Electronics. 1994. *Motorola: A Journey Through Time and Technology*. Schaumburg, IL: Motorola University Press.

————. 1997 "Motorola During World War II." Schaumburg, IL.

Mullin, Tom (ed.). 1993. *The Nature of Chaos*. Oxford: Clarendon Press.

Murphy, Dan. 1977. *Lewis and Clark: Voyage of Discovery*. Las Vegas: KC Publications.

————. 1992. *Oregon Trail, Voyage of Discovery: The Story Behind the Scenery*. Las Vegas: KC Publications.

Naisbett, John, and Patricia Aburdene. 1990. *Megatrends 2000*. New York: Avon Books.

Nature. "What the Ancients Believed." November 3, 1994. p. 17.

Nature. "One Discovery Inside Another." November 3, 1994. p. 19.

Nelson, Emily, and Joseph B. White. "Kodak Moment Came Fast for CEO Fisher, Who Takes a Stumble." *Wall Street Journal*. July 25, 1997, p. A1.

Newby, Eric. 1975. *The Rand McNally World Atlas of Exploration*. New York: Rand McNally & Company.

Newmarch, Rosa (ed.). 1905. *The Life and Letters of Peter Ilich Tchaikovsky*. New York: Dodd, Mead & Co.

Ogilvy, David. 1983. *Ogilvy on Advertising*. New York: Crown Publishers.

Ohmae, Kenichi. 1982. *The Mind of the Strategist*. New York: Penguin Books.

Omni Magazine. "Norman Packard." January 1992, p. 85–97.

Ornstein, Robert. 1986. *Multimind: A New Way of Looking at Human Behavior*. New York: Anchor Books.

Osborne, David, and Ted Gaebler. 1992. *Reinventing Government*. New York: Plume.

Overbye, Dennis. "The Cosmos According to Darwin." *The New York Times Magazine*. July 13, 1997, p. 24–27.

Pais, Abraham. 1994. *Einstein Lived Here*. New York: Oxford University Press.

Peat, F. David. 1993. "Science as Story." In *Sacred Stories*. Charles Simpkinson and Anne Simpkinson (eds.). HarperSanFrancisco.

Peitgen, Heinz-Otto, Hartmut Jürgens, and Dietmar Saupe. 1992. *Chaos and Fractals: New Frontiers of Science.* New York: Springer-Verlag.

Peitgen, H.-O., and P. H. Richter. 1986. *The Beauty of Fractals: Images of Complex Dynamical Systems.* New York: Springer-Verlag.

Penrose, Roger. 1989. *The Emperor's New Mind.* New York: Oxford University Press.

Perls, Frederick S., Ralph F. Hefferline, and Paul Goodman. 1951. *Gestalt Therapy.* New York: Julian Press.

Peters, Thomas J., and Robert H. Waterman. 1982. *In Search of Excellence.* New York: Warner Books.

Peters, Tom. 1987. *Thriving on Chaos.* New York: Alfred A. Knopf.

———. "The Search for Excellence Continues." *Forbes.* December 2, 1996, p. 239–40.

Peterson, Ivars. "The Color of Geometry." *Science News.* December 23/30, 1989, p. 408–15.

Pickover, Clifford A. 1990. *Computers, Pattern, Chaos and Beauty.* New York: St. Martin's Press.

———. 1991. *Computers and the Imagination.* New York: St. Martin's Press.

———. 1994. *Chaos in Wonderland: Visual Adventures in a Fractal World.* New York: St. Martin's Press.

———. 1994. "Introduction," In *Frontiers of Scientific Visualization.* Clifford A. Pickover and Stuart K. Tewksbury (eds.). New York: John Wiley & Sons.

Porter, Eliot, and James Gleick. 1990. *Nature's Chaos.* New York: Viking.

Porter, Michael E. 1980. *Competitive Strategy.* New York: The Free Press.

———. 1985. *Competitive Advantage.* New York: The Free Press.

———. "What is Strategy?" *Harvard Business Review.* November–December 1996, p. 61–78.

Prigogine, Iyla. 1984. *Order Out of Chaos: Man's New Dialogue with Nature.* New York: Bantam Books.

———. 1997. *The End of Certainty.* New York: The Free Press.

Proust, Marcel. 1923. *La Prisonnière (Sodome et Gomorrhe, III).* Paris: Nouvelle Revue Francaise.

Reich, Robert B. 1991. *The Work of Nations.* New York: Alfred A. Knopf.

Reimer, Bennett, and Ralph A. Smith (eds.). 1992. *The Arts, Education and Aesthetic Knowing. Part II.* Chicago: The National Society for the Study of Education. Distributed by University of Chicago Press.

Robbins, Tom. 1976. *Even Cowgirls Get the Blues.* Boston: Houghton Mifflin.

Roberts, Johnnie L., John J. Keller, Leslie Cauley, and Mark Robichaux. *Wall Street Journal.* "Bell Atlantic's Pact to Acquire TCI Collapses Amid Dispute Over Price." February 24, 1994, p. A3–6.

Ronda, James P. "Imaging the West Through the Eyes of Lewis & Clark." *We Proceeded On.* May 1992. Great Falls, MT: Lewis and Clark Trail Heritage Foundation.

Rowe, Alan J., Richard O. Mason, Karl E. Dickel, Richard B. Mann, and Robert J. Mockler. 1994. *Strategic Management: A Methodological Approach*. New York: Addison-Wesley.

Ruelle, David. 1991. *Chance and Chaos*. Princeton: Princeton University Press.

Ruthen, Russell. "Adapting to Complexity." *Scientific American*. January 1993, p. 128–40.

Salter, Christopher L., Gail L. Hobbs, and Cathy Salter. 1995. *Key to the National Geography Standards*. Washington, DC: National Geographic Society.

Schattschneider, Doris. "Escher's Metaphors." *Scientific American*. November 1994, p. 68.

Schroeder, Manfred. 1991. *Fractals, Chaos, Power Laws: Minutes from an Infinate Paradise*. New York: W.H. Freeman.

Schwartz, Peter, and Kevin Kelly. "The Relentless Contrarian." *Wired*. August 1996.

Scientific American. Mind and Brain. Special Issue. September 1992.

Scientifc American. Mysteries of the Mind. Special Issue. 1997.

Senge, Peter M. 1990. *The Fifth Discipline*. New York: Currency and Doubleday.

Shapin, Steven. 1996. *The Scientific Revolution*. Chicago: The University of Chicago Press.

Sheldrake, Rupert. 1988. *The Presence of the Past*. New York: Vintage Books.

———. 1991. *The Rebirth of Nature*. New York: Bantam Books.

Shekerjian, Denise. 1990. *Uncommon Genius: How Great Ideas are Born*. New York: Viking.

Siler, Todd. 1990. *Breaking the Mind Barrier*. New York: Touchstone.

———. 1996. *Think Like a Genius*. Englewood, CO: ArtScience Publications.

Smart, Tim. "Jack Welch's Encore." *BusinessWeek*. October 2, 1996, p. 154–60.

Smolin, Lee. 1997. *The Life of the Cosmos*. New York: Oxford University Press.

Snyder, Gary. 1990. *The Practice of the Wild*. San Francisco: North Point Press.

Soros, George. "The Capitalist Threat." *Atlantic Monthly*. February 1997.

Stewart, Ian. 1995. *Nature's Numbers*. New York: BasicBooks.

Stewart, Ian, and Martin Golubitsky. 1992. *Fearful Symmetry: Is God a Geometer?* New York: Penguin Books.

Stott, Carole. 1995. *Celestial Charts*. London: Studio Editions.

Strayer, Joseph R. (ed. in chief). 1989. *Dictionary of the Middle Ages. Vol. 3*. New York: Charles Scribner's Sons.

Suzuki, David, and Peter Knudtson. 1992. *Wisdom of the Elders*. New York: Bantam Books.

Sykes, Christopher. 1994. *No Ordinary Genius*. New York: W.W. Norton.

Talbot, Michael. 1991. *The Holographic Universe*. New York: HarperCollins.

Tesla, Nikola. 1982. *My Inventions*. Williston, VT: Hart Brothers.

Tichy, Noel, and Mary Anne Devanna. 1986. *The Transformational Leader*. New York: John Wiley & Sons.

Toffler, Alvin. 1985. *The Adaptive Corporation*. New York: Bantam Books.

———. 1990. *Powershift*. New York: Bantam Books

Tourtellot, Jonathan B. (ed.). 1987. *Into the Unknown: The Story of Exploration*. Washington, DC: National Geographic Society.

Tufte, Edward R. 1997. *Visual Explanations*. Cheshire, CT: Graphics Press.

Tzu, Sun. Thomas Cleary (trans.). 1988. *The Art of War*. Boston: Shambala.

Ulam, Adam B. 1992. *The Communists: The Story of Power and Lost Illusions 1948–1991*. New York: Charles Scribner's Sons.

Waldrop, M. Mitchell. 1992. *Complexity: The Emerging Science at the Edge of Order and Chaos*. New York: Touchstone.

Waterman, Jr., Robert H. 1987. *The Renewal Factor*. New York: Bantam Books.

Watts, Alan. 1957. *The Way of Zen*. New York: Vintage Books.

Watzlawick, Paul. 1984. *The Invented Reality*. New York: W.W. Norton.

Weinberg, Neil. "New Age Documents." *Forbes*. June 6, 1994, p. 75.

Weisbord, Marvin. 1987. *Productive Workplaces*. San Francisco: Jossey-Bass.

West, Thomas. 1991. *In the Mind's Eye*. Buffalo: Prometheus Books.

Westfall, Richard S. 1971. *The Construction of Modern Science*. New York: John Wiley & Sons.

Wetherell, W. D. "Point North. Uhhh . . ." *New York Times*. May 5, 1996, p. xx 35.

White, Michael, and John Gribben. 1992. *Stephen Hawking: A Life in Science*. New York: Dutton.

Wiggins, Stephen. 1990. *Introduction to Applied Nonlinear Dynamical Systems and Chaos*. New York: Springer-Verlag.

Wilber, Ken (ed.). 1982. *The Holographic Paradigm and Other Paradoxes*. Boston: Shambala.

Wilber, Ken. 1996. *A Brief History of Everything*. Boston: Shambala.

Wilford, John Noble. "In a Golden Age of Discovery Faraway Worlds Beckon." *New York Times*. February 9, 1997, p. A-1.

Wycoff, Joyce. 1991. *Mindmapping: Your Personal Guide to Exploring Creativity and Problem-Solving*. New York: Berkley Books.

Yankelovish, Daniel. 1981. *New Rules*. New York: Random House.

Yam, Philip. "Bringing Schrödinger's Cat to Life." *Scientific American*. June 1997, p. 124–29.

Young, James Webb. 1975. *A Technique for Producing Ideas*. Chicago: Crain Communications.

Zinker, Joseph. 1977. *Creative Process in Gestalt Therapy*. New York: Vintage Books.

Zukav, Gary. 1979. *The Dancing Wu Li Masters*. New York: Bantam Books.

ACKNOWLEDGMENTS

The beauty of the new science is it that allows the traveler to find his or her way back to the creative, dynamic, natural processes of life. And I feel a deep appreciation for those who have supported my journey.

This book would not have been written without the constant support and encouragement of my friend, former spouse, and political maverick, John Yoder. With his honest, kind, and good-natured temperament, John helped me find my way when I felt lost, and regain a healthy perspective when I was caught up in the drama and seriousness of it all. And his comments and suggestions on the manuscript strengthened the book immeasurably.

Janet Coleman, my first editor, nurtured this book from its beginning. Without her there would be no book. Stephen Morrow guided the manuscript through its final stages and into production. I am grateful to him for his editorial skills and gentle nature, which allowed me to hand over my creative child with confidence.

Special acknowledgment goes to Dr. Edward N. Lorenz, whose pioneering work brought chaos theory into focus. Without his work, recognition of the order hidden within the seemingly random behavior of a nonlinear system would have taken much longer.

I still remember the day I walked into the Jefferson Building in Washington, DC, the old Library of Congress building, and waited in a quiet, dark, and beautifully ornate area for a copy of his 1963 article from the *Journal of the Atmospheric Sciences*. When the librarian handed me the article, I remember feeling that I had just been given a treasure map, a guide to something that would have great meaning in my life.

In a recent telephone conversation, Dr. Lorenz offered to provide an original version of the Lorenz Attractor for this book. My conversation with him, his gracious offer, and the pictures he provided were the highlights of this entire effort.

Walter LaMendola has been a friend since the day we met. Through his own writing experiences, he knew about the dark days that lay ahead of me as I began the process of writing this book. And when the darkness descended, he was always there to remind me that I wasn't alone and that it would pass. Our visits over coffee always stimulated my thinking, and in his wonderful Sicilian way he would remind me to take a deep breath and appreciate the fullness of life.

Lawrence Hudetz, whose photographs appear in this book, has been a constant touchstone through the last year. His in-depth knowledge about the new science and the experience of working with me as a partner, gave his comments a wisdom and a subtlety that gracefully set me back on track when a detour seemed more appealing.

Without the urging of Judy Hayes Ellison to read James Gleick's 1987 book, *Chaos: Making a New Science*, I would not have found this path as soon as I did. We have been friends for more than a decade, and through the years Judy has taught me a great deal about life, Africa, and the field of future studies. And through her project on child sexual abuse, *Tears of the Children*, we have explored the value of art in helping individuals reveal the emotional and psychological wounds of abuse, and in bringing the interrelatedness of issues into clearer focus.

As a business professor and systems thinker, John Landry has shared an enthusiasm for my work and its potential benefits. And his astute and generous nature sent a constant stream of books and articles my way.

Six special friends—Phyllis Casavant and Gayle Kenny, whom I have known since my college days; Suzanne Ingram, a childhood friend; Dottie Keville and Jane Burke, friends from Washington, DC; and, Stephanie West Allen, one of the first people I met in Colorado—are sisters and kindred spirits. Their support, insight, willingness to help, and good humor were always just a telephone call away.

Tom Gray, now retired from the National Park Service (NPS) and traveling the country with his camera, sat with me in the theater at the NPS's Audio-Visual Center in Harpers Ferry, WV, and helped me select fractal images from the slide shows used to introduce visitors to each of our national parks. Several of his beautiful photographs are found in this book.

The film librarians at the headquarters for the National Aeronautics and Space Administration (NASA) in Washington, DC, trusted me enough to leave me alone in a room filled with file cabinets of pictures taken by astronauts and the cameras mounted aboard NASA's space shuttle missions. What a treat!

Archie Brodsky, Pat Read, and Nick Taylor helped me navigate the intricacies of the publishing world. The artistic touches of Karen Groves gave a polished look to my promotional materials and the illustrations found in this book. The photographic skill and patience of Lisa Griffin gave me a range of choices for the book jacket photograph. And a photograph from her personal collection appears in the section of the book on fractals.

The research for this book could not have been completed without the responsive and thorough assistance I received from the reference librarians at the Evergreen Branch of the Jefferson County (CO) Public Library. And comments from individuals who attended my speaking engagements as well as my workshops and seminars, including those for the World Future Society and at Esalen Institute, added ideas, concrete suggestions, and a variety of perspectives, which strengthened the presentation of the information found in this book.

And finally, writing this book has given me many opportunities to find unexpected meaning in new relationships, and to reconnect with old friends and colleagues. In Washington, DC and around the world: Venus Andrecht, Phyllis Arrington, Maryann Beck, Don Burke, David Casella, John Francis, Robert "Jake" Jacobs, David May, Keith Miles,

Dorothea Musgrave, Anna Lawrence Ohlson, Jerry O'Kungu, Charlie Seashore, Larry Serviolo, Stan Shulman, and Paula Weiss-Martin. In Colorado: Pat Brewster, Maria Cook and Steve Millenson, Doug Easterling, Alysia and Tim Kehoe, Ken Kullhem, Barbara and George Long, Judith McCabe, Peter Moogk, Lynn Parker, Nina Sampsel, Maureen Spiegleman, Denise Stoner, Pam and Hal Warren, and Amy and Jim White.

To each and all, thank you!

INDEX

ABOUT THE AUTHOR

Since 1989, Irene Sanders has pioneered the application of the new science of chaos theory and complexity to the much-needed skill of strategic thinking. Today, as principal of Sanders & Company, she helps organizations of all types see, understand, and influence the dynamics of the real world context in which their decisions are being made.

She frequently provides strategic thinking and planning services to individual members and committees of the United States Congress. In 1989–90, she served as personal consultant to the secretary of the U.S. Department of Health and Human Services. She served as director of marketing and public affairs for the National Rehabilitation Hospital located in Washington, DC; originated and hosted a series for public television; and served as legislative assistant to U.S. Senator Sam Nunn. She is a graduate of Duke University and the Medical College of Georgia, and she completed a fellowship in organizational change at Johns Hopkins University.

Her life and work have been fueled by an intense curiosity and optimism about people, politics, and the ways in which individuals and organizations make positive contributions in the world. And her lifelong interests in art, science, and world events have resulted in many innovative and collaborative firsts.

She has been involved as a board member, consultant, or manager in the design and start-up phases of more than a dozen organizations. And following an early 1990 trip to Eastern Europe, she developed a model used jointly by the U.S. Department of State and the U.S. Department of Health and Human Services to help citizens of the former Soviet Union manage the impact of political change.

She has worked with a wide range of Fortune 500 companies, international groups, and nonprofit organizations. And this book represents her belief that in a world where many struggle just to survive, it's important to remember that there are "patterns which connect"* all of creation to the creative and compassionate heart of humanity.

She was born in Atlanta, GA, spent twelve years in Washington, DC, and now lives in Evergreen, CO, with her four-legged children, Flossie and Zack (Old English sheepdogs) and a herd of elk who graze in the backyard.

Irene Sanders, P.O. Box 2856, Evergreen, CO 80437-2856

Phone: 303-674-0734 Fax: 303-674-8188

e-mail: irene @ sandersco.com